DET

EVALUATING THE BENEFITS OF LIFELONG LEARNING

The Centre for Research on the Wider Benefits of Learning
Institute of Education
20 Bedford Way
London WC1H 0AL
020 7612 6902
website: *http://www.learningbenefits.net*
email: *info@learningbenefits.net*

EVALUATING THE BENEFITS OF LIFELONG LEARNING
A Framework

Ian Plewis and John Preston

Centre for Research on the Wider Benefits of Learning
Institute of Education | Birkbeck College

First published in 2001 by the Institute of Education,
University of London, 20 Bedford Way, London WC1H 0AL

Pursuing Excellence in Education

© Institute of Education, University of London 2001

British Library Cataloguing in Publication Data
A catalogue record for this publication is available from the
British Library

ISBN 0 85473 656 5

Cover and text design by Tim McPhee
Page make-up by Cambridge Photosetting Services, Cambridge
Production services by Book Production Consultants plc,
Cambridge
Printed by Watkiss Studios, Biggleswade

Contents

Tables

Figures

Preface

The Centre for Research on the Wider Benefits of Learning was established in 1999 by the then Department for Education and Employment, now the Department for Education and Skills (DfES). The Centre's task is to investigate the non-economic benefits that learning brings to the individual learner and to society as a whole. This is a joint initiative between the Institute of Education and Birkbeck College, University of London.

This paper covers a range of issues that need to be considered when researchers and others are setting up evaluations of interventions in the life-long learning area. Evaluation is a broad term that can encompass a variety of activities. Our focus in this paper is on estimating the impact of interventions on learners, their families and the communities in which they live, an activity sometimes known as summative evaluation. We do, however, also consider formative, or process, evaluation and outline some ideas about how the two approaches can be used to complement each other. We also illustrate how impact evaluation can be linked to those economic methods known generically as Cost-Benefit Analysis.

We would like to thank Professor John Bynner, Director of the Centre for Longitudinal Studies, colleagues in the Centre for Research on the Wider Benefits of Learning, and Sue Stone and her colleagues in the former Department for Education and Employment for helpful comments on earlier versions of this paper.

Chapter 1

Introduction

Evaluation is a key tool of policy. Without it the realisation of policy goals remains uncertain, with judgements made about success and failure relying as much on hunch and intuition as on hard evidence. The implementation of government policies embodied in the Green Paper *The Learning Age*, (DfEE, 1998a) and the subsequent White Paper *Learning to Succeed* (DfEE, 1999a) are no exceptions.

This report sets out the key principles that underpin effective evaluations as applied to policy initiatives in the field of lifelong learning and the variety of methods that are available to implement them.

Lifelong learning policies have recently been classified under four headings (Hillage et al., 2000):

- *Changes to the learning infrastructure*: for example, replacing the Further Education Funding Council (FEFC) and Training and Enterprise Councils (TEC) by the Learning and Skills Council (LSC) and the introduction, in 1998 of the electronically based National Grid for Learning (NGfL).

- *Changes to partnership and brokerage arrangements:* for example, promoting Learning Partnerships (LP) to co-ordinate provider activities with purchaser demand and the development of the role of the University for Industry (UfI) as a broker of on-line learning materials through the **learndirect** brand.
- *Changes in provider arrangements:* that is the proposed changes in the funding and inspection regimes for providers.
- *Policy initiatives:* for example, the Adult and Community Learning Fund, IT Learning Centres, Career Development Loans, Workforce Development Fund, Union Learning Fund, Family Learning and Numeracy, Basic Skills Initiatives and Individual Learning Accounts. Each of these policies has a range of aims, as illustrated in Chapter 3 (Figure 3.2).

These four areas usefully delineate the boundaries of our evaluation studies, which span changes in institutional arrangements, student support and curriculum. The common thread is 'Lifelong Learning', both as an end in itself and the means of achieving the wider set of benefits. What do we mean by lifelong learning? Bagnall (1990) offers four overlapping definitions:

- The distribution of formal education and training throughout an individual's lifespan;
- The educative function of the whole of one's life experience, making particular reference to the informal aspects of learning;
- The preparation of individuals for the management of their adult lives, stressing the purposes of learning;
- The identification of education with the whole of life – a holistic approach to the concept.

In this report, we will be placing more emphasis on the formal aspects of lifelong learning, in particular post-compulsory education and training in all its forms and at all ages. The wider benefits include improved health, greater civic participation and less crime.

SCOPE OF THE REPORT

Our focus is on *methods* for evaluating the effects of the range of policy interventions and programmes in the area of lifelong learning. We are less explicitly concerned with evaluation 'theories' although these theories do, of course, inform much of what we write and we refer to them as appropriate. Nor do we say anything about how the interventions themselves should be developed and designed, and what their initial aims and objectives should be. It is, however, possible that the nature of a programme might change as a result of evaluation.

We distinguish evaluation from monitoring in the next section. Evaluation is fundamentally concerned with the controls exercised through the research design. We also give some attention to modelling observational (i.e. survey) data for estimating the overall effects of lifelong learning, in which control through design gives way to statistical control. We also consider how economic outcomes can be estimated for interventions. In the third section, we set out a classification of the kinds of policies and programmes that could, in principle, be evaluated.

In Chapter 2, we examine the types of evaluation that are applicable to lifelong learning, illustrated by examples from the literature. We consider both qualitative and quantitative approaches in this chapter, although the report as a whole leans more towards quantitative methods. Chapter 3 gives an overview of measuring relevant outcomes, both learning outcomes and their wider benefits. This is, however, a broad area that goes beyond evaluation and is covered in more detail in the first paper in this series by Schuller et al. (2001). Impact evaluation is covered in Chapters 4 and 5 with Chapter 4 focusing more on research design and Chapter 5 more on statistical analysis. Chapter 6 shows how cost-benefit analysis can be used to provide an economic assessment of interventions. We end in Chapter 7 with some conclusions and recommendations. Throughout the report, we provide contexts for evaluation work in terms of hypothetical but plausible examples.

MONITORING, MODELLING AND EVALUATION

In this section, we draw some distinctions between three different kinds of activity: monitoring, evaluation and modelling. The benefits of lifelong learning can be assessed in a number of ways. We might, for example, hypothesise that more learning in the adult population under the age of 30 would lead to better health outcomes in middle age. More specifically, we might suppose that learning could lead to lower age-specific rates for cigarette smoking (and hence to concomitant reductions in certain age-specific disease rates). One way of testing this hypothesis would be, first, to find out whether successive cohorts from this age group were, in fact, exhibiting greater levels of learning and, second, to find out whether smoking rates were declining for the same cohorts. In other words, learning and smoking rates could each be *monitored* over time, by drawing on data from administrative sources and from repeated surveys. Evidence of an increasing learning rate and a declining smoking rate over the same period would be consistent with the causal hypothesis – especially if there were a clear discontinuity in the 'time series' soon after the learning initiative was introduced (Cook and Campbell, 1979).

Such a monitoring exercise would not, however, be regarded as a rigorous test of the effects of learning on smoking in that the data only demonstrate an association between the two variables. Moreover, this association would be between rates at the aggregate level rather than between measured behaviours at the individual level – and it is individuals who learn and who give up smoking. Consequently, the association would be open to a variety of interpretations. It would not be possible to conclude that smoking rates had declined *because* learning had increased and even less plausible to assert that smoking had declined because of government policies designed to encourage and increase learning. On the other hand, evidence obtained from monitoring exercises of the kind just described can be useful. First, if the evidence were consistent with the hypothesis then this would be a reason for a more intensive and rigorous exploration of any direct link. Second, if the trend in smoking rates were not consistent with the hypothesis, this would suggest that policies were not having the desired effect, at least as far as smoking was concerned. In other words, monitoring can establish the necessary, but not the *sufficient* conditions for establishing a causal effect.

Monitoring as just described may therefore assist in judging the effectiveness of policy, but it is not evaluation in the full sense of the term. (Note that we use the term 'monitoring' rather differently from some authors, for example, Rossi and Freeman, 1993, who use it to describe what we call, in Chapter 2, implementation evaluation.) In the sense used here, evaluation is a *research* activity that draws on principles of research design and measurement in social science to establish as unequivocally as possible that a change in a targeted outcome of an intervention can be attributed to the intervention rather than to some other unobserved factor or factors. This inevitably requires building into the design various kinds of *controls*. Generally, statistical methods are used in order to try to test the (causal) hypothesis concerning the intervention, and to estimate the size of its hypothesised effect. Qualitative methods are also often used to illuminate the processes involved.

Importantly, evaluation is, or should be, a planned activity rather than a haphazard, and often belated response to an initiative of some kind. Evaluations that are bolted on to an intervention that is already in operation are less likely to be useful than evaluations where the design has been integrated into the development of the intervention before it fully begins.

In Chapter 2, we go into more detail about the kinds of evaluation approaches and methods that would be appropriate when evaluating a life-long learning initiative. These include formative, illuminative and realistic evaluation on the more qualitative side, and summative and impact evaluation, which are more quantitative in nature. We show how the different approaches to evaluation can be linked by studies of the process of change, and how these draw on the variability in the way interventions are implemented. Heterogeneity is a particularly important issue in the evaluation of educational interventions. Also, in Chapter 2, we contrast the social science approach to evaluation with ideas that are more familiar in management.

Located somewhere between monitoring and evaluation, there is a third way of assessing the benefits of lifelong learning. With this approach, data, ideally longitudinal data, are collected from a sample of the target population. The relation between individuals' learning experiences and their subsequent smoking behaviour, for example, is then *modelled* in a statistical sense. That is to say the controls applied are statistical, enabling us to gauge the effect of one variable on another (the outcome) taking account of the effects of all other variables with which the variable of interest might be *confounded*. For example, giving up smoking might be more common among men than women or among the more rather than the less educated and is nothing to do with the learning intervention itself. Often, all we can do is to model observational data in this way to get some purchase on evidence relevant to the hypothesis in question because planned evaluations are not practicable. But there will always be difficulties in establishing causal inferences about policies and programmes from this kind of modelling, not least because individuals with particular characteristics (that we have not measured) select themselves into learning and, possibly, out of smoking. Longitudinal data are helpful because they do, at least, provide information on time sequencing but they cannot eliminate the endemic problems generated by self-selection. We return to these problems in Chapters 4, 5 and 6.

As already stated, our focus in this report is on evaluation rather than on modelling, and less on monitoring. However, we recognise that the boundaries between these three activities are not clearly drawn. For example, as noted earlier the 'interrupted time series design' is a form of monitoring that has been used for evaluation (Cook and Campbell, 1979, Ch. 4). With this design, discontinuities in a time series observed to coincide with a policy change (for example, rate of use of seatbelts) are matched to any discontinuities in the expected effect of the policy change (fatality rates from traffic accidents).

In Appendix 1.1, we outline which official statistics and other secondary data might be used to monitor learning changes and their wider benefits over time. We also show how modelling can be used in conjunction with evaluation methods, when assessing the costs and benefits of a policy change. As we pointed out earlier, the defining characteristic of an evaluation study is that it is designed as such from the outset, with the aim of finding out whether and how the intervention is working, and what its effects are.

CLASSIFYING INTERVENTIONS

Many educational policies and, more particularly, changes in those policies, result in interventions in the sense that, ultimately, they aim to affect learning. Consequently, we use the term 'intervention' as shorthand for a variety of policies and programmes.

For the purposes of the report we can classify interventions along two dimensions – the people they are aimed at or are available for, and their intended primary outcomes, as proposed by the designers of the intervention.

For the first dimension, we can place interventions into six categories:

1) *Provision available to and experienced by everyone.* Here, the National Curriculum for 5–16 year olds can be seen as an intervention. Evaluating the effects of these kinds of interventions is especially difficult because, by definition, there are no control groups or, more precisely, no contemporaneous control groups. It is, however, sometimes possible to exploit variability in the quality of the provision to obtain some insights into its implementation and effectiveness.

2) *Provision available to anyone but not used by everyone.* This includes

education and training for the 16–18 age group and many of the initiatives set out in Hillage et al. (2000). Interventions falling into this group are also difficult to evaluate because those who use the provision are self-selected. It is extremely difficult to separate out the effects of choice or, more precisely, the characteristics and motivations of those individuals making that choice, from the effects of the provision itself. As more and more of the 16–18 age group are involved in some kind of education so the problems of self-selection in that context become more marked, because those not involved become more and more unusual.

3) *Provision restricted to those who qualify for it but not used by all who qualify.* Higher education is one example, where the restrictions are prior educational attainment and, to an extent, income. Self-selection is also an issue here.

4) *Provision that is restricted by, for example, area.* LEA policies differ in terms of, say, the extent to which they provide adult education or non-mandatory grants. It can also be restricted by industrial sector: the Union Learning Fund is only available to some employees in Trade Unions. Opportunities for more rigorous evaluation are greater in these circumstances because self-selection at the individual level can be less severe.

5) *Provision that is restricted because demand exceeds supply.* For example, the government might introduce a policy to provide free 'Introduction to the Internet' courses for all who would like them, based on estimate of likely take-up. If this estimate is too low then some kind of rationing is needed, and opportunities for evaluation, perhaps based on random assignment, are enhanced.

6) *Provision which is deliberately introduced in an 'experimental' or 'pilot' form.* One example is Education Maintenance Allowances (EMA). Often this will mean that some areas receive the intervention while others do not. In these circumstances, it is, at least in principle, possible to build evaluation into the provision from the outset.

Possible effects of interventions falling into category 1 will generally be monitored, those falling into categories 2 and 3 will usually be modelled whereas those in categories 4, 5 and 6 can, in principle, be evaluated in the sense used in this report.

The second dimension – intended outcomes – can be sub-divided into:

1) *Interventions directly related to learning,* for example, UfI and the University of the Third Age.

2) *Interventions less directly related to the process of learning,* for example, providing EMAs and Individual Learning Accounts.

It is not usually the case that the primary intended outcomes of interventions are the wider benefits of learning. It is also possible for an intervention to have unintended outcomes which might or might not be beneficial for those receiving it. For group 1 there is at least one further step beyond learning to the wider benefits thereof, for group 2 at least two further steps. This raises problems for evaluation in that the severity of self-selection effects is likely to be proportional to the number of steps. For example, take-up of EMAs is likely to be correlated with motivation to learn. It is possible that increased learning in the group receiving EMAs might lead them to vote more often. But propensity to vote will also be influenced by the learner's parents' voting behaviour. Hence, self-selection operates at both stages of a process which might link incentives to learn to civic participation.

SUMMARY

This chapter sets out the main issues covered in the report. The distinction between monitoring, modelling and evaluation, and the classification of interventions, help to define the scope of the report. Appendix 1.1 covers statistical sources for monitoring lifelong learning.

Chapter 2

Types and Styles of Evaluation in Lifelong Learning

There are two parts to this chapter. The first four sections discuss approaches to evaluation that are located within the social science literature, illustrated with examples from the lifelong learning literature. The following two sections consider evaluation methods that have more of a management perspective. The final section brings together the similarities and differences between these two approaches to evaluation.

INTRODUCTION AND OVERVIEW

This chapter and Chapter 3 are shaped by Cronbach's view that a good evaluation design should be multi-faceted. By this, he means that it should have both quantitative (or scientific) and qualitative (or humanistic or illuminative) elements; that it might contain both experimental and naturalistic components; and that it should serve both formative and summative goals (Cronbach, 1982).

Formative evaluation is the process of using evidence to re-direct and improve an intervention (in the generic sense used in Chapter 1, p. 6) in the course of carrying it out. Summative evaluation is directed to judgements about the impact of the intervention overall, that is, its added value over what preceded it. We need to be able to establish that any wider benefits of lifelong learning – improved health in old age, for example – are the result of the intervention rather than just being ascribed to improvements in health generally.

Cronbach argues that formative evaluation is in some ways the more important of the two, not least because as soon as an intervention is implemented it evolves in relation to the local and national context. The evolution can be haphazard, subject to personal or political pressures, and based on unsystematic evidence. Formative evaluation collects and supplies back diagnostic data systematically collected, together with conclusions about what is working and what isn't for which sections of the target population.

Campbell (1988), on the other hand, gives more importance to summative evaluation. Certainly, many interventions involve substantial public expenditure, which means that summative judgements about them at certain points are critical to the policy process surrounding them. We need to know whether a given intervention justifies the money being spent on it. This judgement leads directly to a set of policy options for the future of the intervention:

- whether it should continue or be terminated;
- whether it should be replaced by something different and possibly better;
- whether, if appropriate, its success merits extension to a wider target population.

In addition, evaluation should be conducted in terms of the aims and objectives set out by the architects of the intervention. This means gathering views from all the 'stakeholders' – learners, teachers and so on. This basic evaluation principle has received considerable attention through its recent restatement in the United States under the title 'theory of change' (Connell and Kubisch, 1998) – (see p. 21). It is a point that is often emphasised in community-level evaluations that frequently make use of qualitative data. For example, Moreland and Lovett (1997) use an ethnographic and case study framework to evaluate the influence of adult education providers on the construction of social capital in Northern Ireland. These evaluators often take an approach that emphasises the voice of participants and the importance of learning within the individual's biography. This approach allows a range of learning benefits through the life-course to be identified and explored, a richness of data that is not so easily obtained with quantitative techniques. On the other hand, detailed event histories can be profitably analysed statistically using event history analysis (Plewis, 1997, Ch. 7).

One example of a participatory approach is Edwards (1986), who evaluated a 'Second Chance to Learn' project in Merseyside. This adult education programme had the objective of developing adults' skills by studying local history, developing study skills and attending writing workshops. There were three research methods used in the evaluation of the course: biographical analysis, interviews and questionnaires. Biographical analysis involves tracing, with the student, key learning events and transitions in their lives in order to explore the reasons for undertaking further learning and the possible benefits which might arise. Although the process is time consuming, it allows the construction of learner typologies which might be useful in assessing the impact of learning in terms of its expected wider benefits. Edwards constructed a simple classification of learners – 'high priority' learners for whom completion and personal benefits are likely, 'low priority' where they are not and 'borderline' where chance and personal circumstances are mediating factors.

As the number of students attending the course each year was small, postal questionnaires could be issued to all 253 former students. Additionally, interviews were conducted with an opportunity sample of 40 students. The response rate to the postal surveys was rather poor, with only 115 replies (45 per cent). The use of both questionnaires and interviews enabled researchers to gain a wide understanding of possible benefits of adult education, such as employment, civic participation, changes in attitude and self-confidence, and improvements in family life. In her summary, Edwards provides a useful checklist of issues which should be addressed in the evaluation of adult education (pp.137–41). In particular, she highlights the problems of measurement which the evaluator faces:

The problems of measuring knowledge are miniscule compared to the difficulties in measuring the growth of confidence or increased involvement in community or trade union activities. For this reason, new kinds of measurement must be developed by the evaluator: ones which are suited to the nature of the course and the resources available.

Edwards, 1986: 139

Some of these issues are addressed in Chapter 3. Like Edwards (1986), the Adult Education and Continuing Development Unit of the Inner London Education Authority (ILEA) (AECDU, 1985) evaluated a community-based adult learning programme using personal interviews. The advantage of this approach was that a much higher response rate was obtained and the validity of data could be checked. In addition, the impact of learning on the family could be ascertained more directly.

The evaluation of any lifelong learning intervention needs to address all the issues concerned with evolution and change alongside those to do with effectiveness. Faced with interventions that often have multiple objectives (outcomes) and multiple forms (heterogeneity), evaluators have sometimes shied away from formal quantitative evaluation in favour of a largely descriptive account. Those responsible for adult education are sometimes sceptical about quantitative approaches, preferring to give priority to concepts of social justice above accountability (Cloonan et al., 1999). It is, however, possible to combine tightly designed impact evaluations with other methods of evaluation, using a range of research techniques and designs. In other words, the right balance can and needs to be struck between formative and summative elements of an evaluation employing an optimal research design with the appropriate mix of research methods within it to ensure that the full range of purposes for it can be met. To try to estimate impact without information about implementation and process is likely to lead to misinterpretation. Equally, to ignore questions about impact is ultimately self-defeating.

There is, therefore, a sequence of questions that need to be addressed in an evaluation:

1) What was the nature of the learner population recruited into a lifelong learning intervention? How far did the recruited population differ from the intended, or target, population?
2) How was the intervention implemented, both nationally and, where appropriate, locally, and how are its goals and strategies evolving?
3) What was the immediate impact of the intervention on learning?
4) What were its longer-term effects and wider benefits, and were there any deleterious effects?
5) What were the particular characteristics of the intervention that made a difference – project features, nature of the implementation, type of area and so on?
6) What were the costs and benefits of the intervention in monetary terms?

One study that addressed at least some of the questions from this sequence was an extensive national evaluation in the US, the National Advisory Council on Adult Education (NACAE) assessment of the Federal Adult Education Act. The purposes of the Federal Adult Education Act were to release funds to state education boards to attempt to deal with the educational deficiencies of 54 million US citizens who lacked a high school diploma. The evaluation (National Advisory Council on Adult Education, 1978) dealt with the following issues:

• staff performance;
• organisational structures;
• impacts on clients;
• costs and benefits.

The monetary benefits of the programme were compared to programme costs. For example, the benefit to the taxpayer of the removal of nearly 19,000 claimants from welfare rolls was $35 million compared to just over $2 million in instruction costs for the group. The productivity benefits of 62,000 individuals who found work was valued at $320 million compared to instruction costs of $7.7 million. Other benefits arising from the programme included the 12,000 participants who received citizenship, the 21,000 who received driving licenses and the 30,000 who registered to vote.

Qualitative research in some states revealed changes in participants' attitudes and behaviours not revealed through the statistical findings. These included increased utilization of community resources, and improvements in the school behaviour, and attitudes towards school, of participants' children. Additionally, administrative effectiveness – the administration of the learning project implemented as a result of the Federal Adult Education Act – was assessed through the use of program theory. This is a branch of evaluation closely related to systems theory (discussed below, pp. 22–4), and asks those involved in programme delivery to articulate the causal processes and assumptions which underlie programme effectiveness. This review revealed areas in which programme effectiveness could be improved.

Such a substantive national evaluation of programme aims and processes is unique in the literature and the NACAE evaluation presents policy makers with a broad assessment of both processes and programme outcomes. The evaluation did not, however, attempt to control for background variables or to match cases. It is, therefore, possible that individual characteristics rather than programme effects were responsible for programme outcomes. The need to control for the possibility of self-selection was realised in a future evaluation, that of the 1982 US Job Training and Partnership Act. Here an experimental design was used for evaluation purposes. Economically disadvantaged youths and adults within the scope of the scheme could apply for selected employment and training programmes. However, applicants were randomly allocated to one of two groups – a control group not allowed access to the programme and a treatment or intervention group with access. As the control group and treatment group did not differ systematically in any other way apart from access, the effect of the programme could be ascertained with greater certainty. The value and ethics of randomisation are discussed in Chapter 4.

EVALUATING IMPLEMENTATION

This is concerned with the history of an intervention – where its origins lie, how it builds on what already went on, and how it was shaped in practice – and with how the intervention is delivered on the ground. It is likely to involve a variety of qualitative and quantitative research methods. The data collected may come from a variety of sources including documents, surveys, interviews and observation. Triangulation of these data sources will be important to ensure reliability and validity.

Detailed description and analysis of implementation – how the intervention is planned and delivered – is critical if we are to understand not only whether it works but discover how and why it works. We need to know not only which elements contribute to particular outcomes but also whether the intervention is feasible and practicable. It is generally not enough to know that changes have taken place (both in learning and in health or civic participation, for example), but also what happens inside 'the black box' which is the intervention. We elaborate on this below, pp. 20–1). It is also important to remember that changes may be seen as both outcomes and processes leading to wider benefits. Changes in learning may be important findings in their own right but could also be part of a process which provides explanations for a further change – in health, say.

Understanding implementation, in addition to measuring outcomes, is thus an essential part of evaluation. Lifelong learning interventions will sometimes consist of a set of local projects, built around a central core, and information about implementation would then assist in:

- classifying projects, by building up a picture of different projects' histories, contexts, styles and mix of learning activities;
- understanding the feasibility and practicability of local implementation;
- tracking how implementation changes and develops over time – as local projects introduce new activities, target or attract new clientele, work out new publicity;
- providing a backdrop to understanding the impact of the intervention on learners, their families, the areas in which they live and the organisations for whom they work;
- understanding change as both process and outcome;
- planning how to evaluate impact or effectiveness.

For example, Jarvis et al. (1997) evaluated a small-scale educational voucher scheme operated under the auspices of the Corporation of London. There were parallels between this scheme and the recently introduced Individual Learning Accounts (ILAs). Vouchers were offered both to adults resident in the City of London and to individuals who worked within its boundaries. Each resident received a voucher with a base value of £40 and further criteria such as age, unemployment or lack of basic skills could enhance this value to a total of £275. For workers, the local authority would provide a training subsidy of £200 provided that individuals and their employers would also each contribute £200. There were three objectives of the voucher scheme:

1) to raise the profile of adult learning amongst residents, workers and employers;
2) to facilitate re-entry into learning;
3) to enable greater choice of opportunities for study.

The evaluators proposed three research questions:

1) what had the residents and workers who received vouchers gained from the scheme?
2) why had others not taken up the vouchers?
3) what had business gained?

A systematic random sample was extracted from 25 per cent of the 1,413 residential voucher holders and, in addition, each of the workers who requested a voucher was contacted. Responses of sampled residents were elicited through a postal survey. In addition to questionnaires, interviews were conducted with 50 residents who had used their vouchers and an opportunity sample of 45 who had not. Additional data were collected from businesses within the City and the LEA. Statistical analysis of the data revealed that significant numbers of learners would not have been able to study part-time without this support. In addition, the elderly had benefited in terms of improved quality of life through learning.

Let us now consider a hypothetical extension of the Jarvis et al. study. Suppose a voucher scheme were put into operation by a substantial number of LEAs rather than just one. Suppose also that each LEA was free to decide on the value of the voucher and was also expected to decide how best to reach the target population of learners in the light of local circumstances. There would, nevertheless, be common national elements to the intervention as set out by DfEE in terms of eligibility (both residents and workers) and in terms of the kinds of courses they could be used for (for example, courses with a vocational element).

A full evaluation of the scheme would be concerned with implementation and impact, and the processes linking them, and would have to take account of the heterogeneity likely to be induced by variation in implementation between LEAs. The implementation side of the evaluation would need to address questions such as:

1) How did LEAs make decisions about the way the scheme was to operate in their area, and how were those decisions informed by any previous experience of voucher schemes?

2) How was the scheme administered – centrally by the LEA, by local colleges etc?

3) What methods were used to inform potential users of the scheme?

4) How did LEAs monitor take-up of the scheme, and how did they respond to this information to introduce changes in its operation?

If there were substantial variation in take-up across LEAs, this would, in turn, have implications for any evaluation of impact.

Similar kinds of questions would need to be addressed if the intervention – perhaps a course of some kind – were to be delivered by institutions such as FE colleges. We would then want to find out about, for example:

1) the qualifications and experience of those teaching the course;

2) how enthusiastically teachers used any materials specifically designed for the course;

3) the teaching methods used.

For example, in terms of the assessment of a national initiative, DfEE (1999b) published the results of TEC evaluations from the piloting of ILAs.

The report draws upon the experience of the 12 ILA development projects funded by the DfEE in 1998/99 and deals solely with implementation issues. The evaluation synthesises the interim evaluations made by each of the TECs in order to identify critical factors necessary for the successful launch of ILAs. These factors are grouped around the administration, marketing and financing of ILAs. Although this evaluation does not concern itself with outcomes, it does identify the critical 'theories of change' necessary if the launch of ILAs is to be successful.

Studies of implementation, rather than impact, highlight the need to investigate institutional and client response to lifelong learning initiatives. Hodkinson and Sparkes (1994) evaluated the implementation of a learning subsidy, Training Credits, through a longitudinal case study involving semi-structured interviews. The use of interviews over time enabled the researchers to monitor changing perceptions of the scheme by clients. In addition, interviews were conducted with stakeholders involved in the scheme. This approach to implementation evaluation sought to identify how far the assumptions of the intervention had been met on both the demand side (through the behaviour of the holders of Training Credits) and on the supply side (from institutional providers). Hodkinson and Sparkes found that individuals issued with Training Credits did not act as informed, empowered consumers and that business and training organisations do not necessarily work as closely as was envisaged. In addition, the importance of informal networks, rather than official intervention, in gaining employment was emphasised.

The creation of qualification schema such as National Vocational Qualifications (NVQ) and General National Vocational Qualifications (GNVQ) in the late 1980s and early 1990s has also been a topic for implementation evaluation. Toye and Vigor (1994) conducted case studies and interviews within six organisations in order to evaluate the implementation of NVQs. Individual and group interviews were conducted with senior managers, line managers, employees and trainees. A postal questionnaire was also used to collect data from employees and trainees in a further nine organisations, in addition to the original six. The response rate to this questionnaire was typically low with only one-third of the 704 issued questionnaires returned. Although the Toye and Vigor evaluation revealed possible barriers and opportunities for implementation arising from various groups in the organisation, its focus on large national employers might have misrepresented the views of employers as a whole.

FEDA (1997) in collaboration with the Institute for Education evaluated the implementation of GNVQs. A short questionnaire was issued to all centres registered to offer GNVQ and from 814 returns a stratified sample of 214 centres was chosen to reflect a representative mix of subjects. Each centre was issued with three questionnaires over a two-year period in order to collect information on enrolment figures, courses offered and curriculum predictions in subsequent years. In the first year, more detailed questionnaires were also issued to subject team leaders. From the original 225 centres, there was a high rate of attrition, with only 79 centres responding to all three questionnaires. The quantitative data enabled a statistical analysis to be conducted of the manner in which GNVQ had been implemented between differing institutions and subjects.

EVALUATING IMPACT

This is concerned with determining as unequivocally as possible whether the intervention has produced its intended effects. There are two questions to consider when evaluating the impact of an intervention:
1) have there been changes in the outcomes of interest?
2) can these changes be attributed to the intervention itself?

We need to know whether the wider benefits of learning are greater than they would have been without the intervention, and we need to know how much greater they are. The first question – about monitoring change (see p. 4) – can be answered with careful measurement. Satisfactory answers to the second (counterfactual) question – about cause – depend on the way the evaluation is designed and this is the subject of Chapter 4. In essence, an impact evaluation will estimate the size of the effects of the intervention on outcomes of interest.

Educational interventions can be successful in the short-term but their effects can dissipate over time, especially during the period after the intervention has ended, when variables other than the learning experience become increasingly important. Plewis (2000a) discusses this issue in the context of Reading Recovery. Often, however, it is the long-term effects – on health, criminality and so on – which bring the greatest benefit both to the individual and to society. If long-term effects are postulated then the evaluation design must incorporate a method that enables at least a sample of the intervention's 'graduates' to be followed up. By far the most convincing way of doing this is to include a longitudinal component to the evaluation so that data from the *same* learners (and perhaps also their families) are collected at time points which are important to the intervention and relevant for the learners. In Chapter 6, we show how the potential long-term benefits of educational vouchers for adult learners can be set against the cost of the scheme.

Payne (1990) conducted a rigorous evaluation of the outcomes arising from adult training programmes for the Training Agency and draws attention to a number of important issues in evaluation design. The design is based upon a stratified sample of 785 trainees who were interviewed in Autumn 1987 and contacted again by post in Spring 1989. These were matched with a sample of 760 adults with similar employment histories but who had not participated in a training scheme recently. In addition, administrative data on 2,710 trainees were used. Sophisticated statistical techniques were employed to ascertain the gender, age and ethnicity profile of trainees compared to the general population, and to assess the impact of training on employment-related outcomes such as duration of unemployment, social mobility and earnings.

This evaluation is unusual in terms of the close attention paid to statistical controls and the emphasis on quantitative method. Payne highlights a number of important issues for future evaluations:

- it was not feasible to use randomisation and so matched pairs of trainees were used as controls;
- a problem of a matched pairs design is that of unobserved heterogeneity. For example, there may be differences in motivation between the trainee and control samples. However, a proxy variable – in this case length of unemployment – may be used as an indicator of motivation to succeed;
- practicalities indicated that the matching was based on a small number of variables, and hence the evaluation used multivariate techniques that allowed all relevant measurable differences between the trainee and the control sample to be taken into account;
- people who had trained at low and high skill levels were under-represented in terms of responses to the postal questionnaire. Other techniques may be needed to elicit responses from these individuals;
- ideally an evaluation should monitor drop-outs;
- qualitative information was a useful adjunct to quantitative data.

More recently, an evaluation of the New Deal for Lone Parents (NDLP)

(DSS, 2000a, 2000b) has addressed some of these concerns about hetero-geneity. The evaluation design incorporated a range of components such as site visits, labour market studies, in-depth interviews, surveys of lone parents, analyses of administrative data, work and benefit histories and an assessment of costs and benefits of the prototype. Heterogeneity was controlled by matching individuals in NDLP areas with comparable individuals in other areas and then comparing outcomes. A total of 4,500 interviews were conducted with the treatment (NDLP) and control (no NDLP) samples. Further follow-up interviews were conducted with people who had participated in the programme and others who had stopped claiming income support. Wider benefits of the programme suggested by qualitative research included an increase in 'work readiness' and self-confidence amongst participants. However, the statistical and cost-benefit analyses showed that the programme effects were related to labour market outcomes rather than to the wider benefits of learning.

INSIDE THE BLACK BOX: LINKING IMPLEMENTATION TO IMPACT

As well as knowing whether or not an intervention has had an effect, we also want to learn why it might have been successful. Which elements, or activities, of the intervention led to positive outcomes? Was the effect a direct one or did it operate through an intervening variable? Essentially, a good evaluation should tell us what works for whom in what circumstances. This could then inform decisions about future policies (see p. 10).

Scriven (1973) developed the idea of 'program theory' to point evaluation in the direction of obtaining more understanding of an intervention's effects, rather than just relying on a crude estimate of impact. Program theory is meant to help evaluators articulate the models on which an intervention is based. This involves interviewing actors and stakeholders involved in the intervention to discover the procedural and institutional arrangements that are implicit for effectiveness. For example, the managing agency of a life-long learning project might hypothesise that an increase in adult education expenditure will indirectly improve the education of children – this is based upon a 'theory' about the relation between expenditure on an adult education intervention and child learning. However, institutions that deliver the interventions might articulate different theories concerning the relationship between funding and expenditure, education and learning, and learning by adults and intergenerational education. Program theory is not dissimilar to the 'theories of change' idea proposed by Connell and Kubisch (1998) which they define as 'a systematic and cumulative study of the links between activities, outcomes and contexts'.

One way of getting inside the black box of an intervention is to build heterogeneity into the design of an intervention by, for example, creating a sizeable number of local interventions, each with their own characteristics, as well as a common core determined centrally. Heterogeneity generates a number of problems in terms of research design (see Chapter 4), but it also creates a number of opportunities when it comes to understanding outcomes. Another way is to ask the various stakeholders why they believe the intervention has or has not worked. Triangulation would then be important to try to reconcile possibly conflicting reports. For example, Siemens (1998), in his evaluation of neighbourhood regeneration schemes in St Louis, made use of various techniques such as participant observation, direct response data, document evaluation and focus groups. Three initial focus groups of community residents and service providers generated a needs assessment and evaluation of the educational programme up to that point. These groups were supplemented by focus groups of teachers and parents. In addition, evaluations were conducted by the University of St Louis. This evaluation framework provided the opportunity for triangulation, an action research perspective and the 'ownership' of the project by the community although an overall quantitative structure for evaluation was still necessary, particularly in the later stages of the project.

In the context of the voucher example discussed above (p. 15), it would be important for those carrying out the evaluation to elicit what theories of change were held by DfEE, by LEAs, and by those charged with delivering the intervention. For example, it might be expected that the voucher scheme would only have an effect for learners in more disadvantaged economic situations. The subsidised courses would be directed at these groups, and they would increase their learning and reap the wider benefits generated by that learning. If, however, the vouchers were used mainly by middle-class learners, who would perhaps have taken up places on a course even without the subsidy, then the intervention is unlikely to have an important effect. In other words, there would be a theory of change but the scheme was not in fact implemented as intended.

THE SYSTEMS APPROACH TO EVALUATING LIFELONG LEARNING

A frequently overlooked approach to the evaluation of lifelong learning is the application of systems theory (see, for example, Easton, 1997, Ch. 4) and related aspects such as business process modelling. (Easton (1997) is the only recent guide to the subject of evaluating adult and non-formal education, and it has a definite slant towards qualitative evaluation of projects based in Less Economically Developed Countries.)

In systems thinking, there are five key elements of any activity:

1) The context in which it takes place, for example, other learning opportunities, the institutional context, the structure of qualifications, the labour market and the background characteristics of the learners. This context could include targets and overarching structures such as the National Education and Training Targets and the Learning and Skills Council.

2) The inputs or resources in terms of teachers, capital and finance.

3) The process or methods by which these inputs are then used, for example in formal or informal instruction, distance or face-to-face learning.

4) Outputs such as qualifications.

5) The outcomes arising from these outputs such as increases in different forms of capital (see Chapter 3), which would then feed back into the environment. For example, an increase in human capital for parents might have an effect on the education of their children.

The above model of evaluation can be set out diagrammatically:

Figure 2.1 A systems model for evaluation purposes

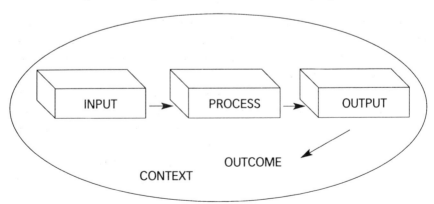

In Figure 2.1 there is a linear relationship between inputs, processes and output although each operates in a wider context. There is the possibility of modelling both recursive (or unidirectional) and circular (or feedback) relationships between elements of the system.

This is obviously a highly generic framework, although even in this unreconstructed form it has some relevance in terms of structuring an evaluation:

- The 'process' domain could be broken down to illustrate funding mechanisms, administrative procedures and learning activities within institutions.
- The 'output' domain could be in terms of numbers of learners completing qualifications, and qualification type.
- The 'outcomes' could be in terms of the creation of human, cultural, social and intellectual capital, changes in attitudes and values, quality of life and macroeconomic variables.
- The 'context' could be the qualifications and institutional structure of post-compulsory learning, and social and economic considerations.

These points are expanded in Chapter 3.

As an example of how a systems approach could be used to model a lifelong learning intervention, see Appendix 2.1 (Easton, 1997: 65). This model shows the expected links between administrative input, instructional processes and post-training outputs of a Non Formal Basic Education adult intervention in the republic of Mali.

An evaluation based on a systems approach involves a comparison of the intervention as planned with the intervention as implemented. The process of evaluation is seen to be continuous and formative, with evaluation results feeding back into the programme structure – the plasticity of the approach allows systems and sub-systems to be re-drafted. Stufflebeam (1971) provides a structure for evaluating interventions of this type (Easton, 1997: 79 – see Appendix 2.2). In Stufflebeam's evaluation framework, the planned intervention is contrasted with the implemented intervention in terms of the context, inputs, processes, impacts and outcomes. Although there is no clearly defined yardstick for measuring the efficacy of the relationship between the planned and implemented attributes of an intervention, systems approaches to evaluation allow for pluralism in terms of research methods.

There are a number of advantages of a systems approach:

1) A system is an instrument that facilitates reflection. The approach has some similarities to the methods of 'realistic evaluation' described by

Pawson and Tilley (1997). Some of the components of the system might be missed in crude statistical or cost-benefit styles of evaluation.

2) Systems evaluations incorporate evaluations of 'theories of change' – the administrative, institutional and individual processes that would need to be in place prior to a change in learning outcomes and wider benefits. They force evaluators to declare systemic links and assumptions. Systems evaluations are frequently combined with program theory in order to give an insider account of key assumptions.

3) Structures and administrative arrangements may be evaluated as key components of the system. In fact, systems evaluations tend to focus on these arrangements. The transition from the FEFC and TECs to the Learning and Skills Council could be evaluated in terms of a systems approach.

There are also disadvantages:

1) It is based on a 'productivist' model of learning. Components are combined in a sequential and systemic fashion in order to arrive at a final outcome. This may not be true of the relationships between lifelong learning and wider benefits.

2) Systems models are predictive, but they are not statistical models of the relationship between inputs, processes and outcomes. However, using statistical methods such as structural equations modelling, relationships between elements of a system and outcomes can be estimated (Caldwell, 1997).

BUSINESS PROCESS MODELS OF EVALUATION

Closely related to systems models of evaluation are those which make use of business processes and concepts in evaluation. In the United Kingdom, NIACE and the University of Birmingham have devised a framework for assessing the 'value added' by 'learning communities'. These communities promote learning widely, develop effective local partnerships between all sectors of the community, and support and motivate individuals and employers to participate in learning (DfEE, 1998b). This toolkit utilises business processes. For example, the value which is produced by services for communities can be broken down into a 'value chain' of inputs / resources, service processes, service outputs, intermediate outcomes and long-term benefits. Analysis of the 'value chain' enables the stakeholders in learning communities to assess the value added by their learning services and to benchmark their services against those of other authorities. Benchmarking is a business practice referring to the measurement of outcomes against those of other organisations. As the process is cyclical, the evaluation feeds into the next planning stage. Table 2.1 gives a proposed evaluation framework.

As Table 2.1 shows, the relation between inputs, processes and outputs is retained from the systems approach to evaluation but the relationships between each are not mapped out in terms of causation. The procedures for evaluation are related to cost-efficiency and the benchmarking of the learning resource against similar facilities in other areas and against previous targets.

Other business–related techniques related to evaluation of lifelong learning include the use of quality circles whereby the workers and management of a learning resource form groups to discuss and improve upon their activities (DfEE, 1999a). This technique is related to concepts of Total Quality Management in Japan and the United States.

CONCLUSION

Systems theory and business process techniques have some uses in evaluation if they are employed alongside other methods. They stress the role played by structures, administration and processes in the linkages between initiating an intervention and its effects on the wider benefits of learning. They are, however, rather similar to the theory of change approach that is central to evaluation. Also, from the quantitative viewpoint that is discussed in more detail in Chapters 4 and 5, relationships are signified but they are neither tested nor estimated. For example, a systems approach to educational interventions might indicate a connection between teacher training and qualification outputs but would not formally test that hypothesis nor estimate the strength of that connection. This is a serious drawback. With regard to qualitative approaches, the use of systems and business terminology could be seen as rather simplistic, masking the depth of interview or case study work.

More generally, this chapter has shown that both quantitative and qualitative methods are needed when evaluating lifelong learning interventions. The organic and unpredictable nature of educational processes and outcomes suggests that interpretative methods such as ethnography, case studies, interviews and individual biography will be useful. On the other hand, estimates

Table 2.1 Analysis of the value chain in learning communities

Inputs	Service process	Service outputs	Outcomes	Benefits	Evaluation of value added
Budget (capital / revenue)	Multi-professional partnership	Courses, training	Learning	Greater opportunities	Clarify purposes
Staff (numbers/ skills)	Collaborative decision making	Library, I.T. resource centre	Skill acquisition/ qualifications	Greater equity for women	Set targets
Materials	User and community involvement in decision making	Creche	Opportunities for job take up	Support of learning needs	Compare achievements with planned targets
Facilities		Advice	Recreation	Child care	Benchmark achievements with other like centres.
		Groups (women's groups, youth club, health awareness campaign group)	Voice: articulation of individual and community needs	Job opportunities	Analyse value added.
		Leisure and recreation facilities	Satisfaction		Analyse cost efficiency (actual and planned costs compared with elsewhere)
					Analyse productive efficiency (relation between inputs and outputs)
					Review against planned objectives

(Adapted from DfEE, 1998b)

26

of impacts on learning and the consequent wider benefits require a quantitative, statistical approach. A good evaluation will combine these two approaches to arrive at a set of conclusions that take account of context, implementation, process and short- and long-term outcomes.

Chapter 3

Outcomes from
Lifelong Learning Interventions

INTRODUCTION

The targets of evaluations are the outcomes interventions attempt to bring about. Has the curriculum change produced a change in pupil performance? Is the establishment of the UfI leading to increased participation in learning? In this chapter, we present a framework for considering such outcomes from the range of lifelong learning policies presented in *The Learning Age* (DfEE, 1998a). In doing so, we propose ways in which the performance of the learning infrastructure (LSCs, NGfL), partnerships and brokers (LPs, UfI), institutions and specific policy initiatives may all be assessed. This discussion will largely cover ways in which policies could be monitored, although there might be some scope for modelling intermediate outputs from interventions. We examine in detail the final outcomes of policy interventions at the individual, family, organisation, community and macro levels. These outcomes are illustrated with indicators that have been used in UK and international contexts. We also consider, as appropriate, intermediate outcomes, which signify the processes through which the ultimate outcomes are achieved.

We distinguish between final and intermediate outcomes (or processes) of lifelong learning interventions. In Figure 3.1 we partition the outcomes of lifelong learning policies using the same breakdown of infrastructure, partnerships/brokers, institutions and policy outcomes that was used in Chapter 1. The first three boxes refer to intermediate outcomes of lifelong learning policies, whereas the last relates to final impacts.

Figure 3.1 Intermediate outcomes and impact of lifelong learning policies

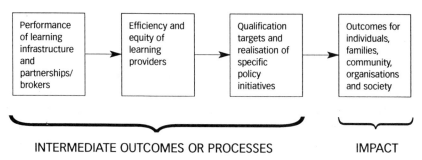

| Performance of learning infrastructure and partnerships/ brokers | Efficiency and equity of learning providers | Qualification targets and realisation of specific policy initiatives | Outcomes for individuals, families, community, organisations and society |

INTERMEDIATE OUTCOMES OR PROCESSES   IMPACT

Figure 3.1 shows how structural changes arising from lifelong learning policies translate, ultimately, into outcomes for individuals, families, communities and society. The intermediate outcomes refer to the performance of key institutions and providers, the achievement of qualification targets and the realisation of specific policy initiatives. The impact of lifelong learning policies refers to measurable outcomes at different levels. This way of thinking about intermediate outcomes and final impacts is related to the styles of evaluation set out in Chapter 2 in that the intermediate outcomes can be regarded as processes that help to explain why there has, or has not been an impact on learners, their families and their communities. Figure 3.1 is also closely related to the systems approach and business process models for evaluation (see Chapter 2).

INTERMEDIATE OUTCOMES

Performance of the learning infrastructure

In Chapter 1 we described the government infrastructure through which resources for learning providers are allocated. In the UK, this consists of the Learning Skills Council (LSC) and the National Grid for Learning (NGfL). The LSC is the overarching body with responsibility for the lifelong learning sector. Therefore, the performance of the LSC could be evaluated with regard to the intermediate and final outputs of the sector as a whole. Key indicators could include:

- Provider efficiency (pp. 31–2)
- Equity (pp. 33–6)
- Qualifications targets and policy implementation (pp. 37–8)
- Learning outcomes (pp. 39–42)

The performance of a learning hub such as the NGfL portal could be evaluated against existing criteria for website and network use. Broad quantitative measures such as the number of times the site is accessed, the number of users, downloads and number of links to the site may provide a guide to the usefulness of the NGfL resource. These may be complemented by more subtle measures of user behaviour such as the number of times a user returns to consult the resource, or the 'surfing' pattern of users on the sites. This provides a guide to what is called the 'stickiness' of the site: the degree to which users remain on and return to NGfL. User feedback is currently assessed through an electronic evaluation form at NGfL. Other qualitative methods of evaluation such as interviews and focus groups could be used to complement this method. (These ideas are illustrative; a full evaluation of NGfL would need to take account of other aspects of the programme.)

Performance of partnerships and brokers

In Chapter 1 we defined partnerships and brokers as co-ordinating and exchanging lifelong learning resources. York Consulting is currently developing a framework for the evaluation of Learning Partnerships for DfEE. The outcomes of this evaluation will identify performance indicators and good practice for the operation of partnerships. It is likely that performance indicators relating to cost-effectiveness will also be specified.

As a broker of learning materials, the University for Industry (UfI) is currently following a business process model of evaluation (see Chapter 2, pp. 24–5). This currently involves market research through accompanied learning, where learners provide feedback about on-line learning materials whilst they work through them. Additionally, customer focus groups are utilised in service assessment (UfI, 2000).

Provider performance

The performance of institutions providing lifelong learning is currently monitored in three ways:

1) By the use of performance indicators and league tables;
2) Through inspection regimes by OFSTED, FEFC, HEFC, Adult Learning Inspectorate and Local Authorities;
3) By internal monitoring and audit by institutions through measurement of value added, implementation of quality management techniques and self-assessment.

We concentrate on the use of performance indicators, although both inspection and internal statistics provide information on provider outcomes.

We distinguish between performance indicators which measure educational efficiency, and those that measure equity. We first outline concepts of efficiency and equity that are commonly used. We then classify current and forthcoming institutional performance indicators according to efficiency and equity considerations. This enables us to ascertain areas where indicators may be lacking. By performance indicators we refer to the range of formal measures by which the performance of institutions is formally judged and ranked by bodies such as the FEFC or HEFCE. These indicators are also used as a basis for funding allocations. However, there are other statistics that can be used to monitor the performance of institutions – see Appendix 1.1.

Institutional efficiency can be conceptualised in four ways (Cohn and Geske, 1990):

1) *Educational output*: such as the number of qualifications awarded.
2) *Educational throughputs*: such as retention or module completion.
3) *Internal efficiency*: the efficiency with which resources are allocated within an educational institution. This is measured in relation to inputs such as cost per graduate.

4) *External efficiency*: the efficiency with which resources are allocated with respect to the 'needs' of society. This is measured in relation to a social output such as graduates in employment. More sophisticated measures of external efficiency such as the private and social rate of return may be calculated (see Chapter 6).

Table 3.1 indicates the range of performance indicators that can be used (or are in use) to measure institutional efficiency, under these four headings, in the FE and HE sectors. As indicated in the table a number of indicators of throughput and output of students in FE are currently in place. Others could be employed.

Table 3.1 Current and proposed performance indicators of the efficiency of lifelong learning providers

Efficiency	Output	Throughput	Internal efficiency	External efficiency
FE indicators in use Source: FEFC (2000)	Achievement of the funding target Achievement rate with regard to learning goals Contribution to the national targets	Change in student numbers In-year retention rate Recruitment and retention of FE students by LEA, College and FEFC region	Out-turn average level of funding (ALF): funding per unit	Achievements and destinations for Colleges in the Further Education Sector (FEFC)
Proposed FE indicators Source: As above	As above, but for mature as well as adult students	As above, but for mature as well as adult students	Value-for-money indicator	As above
HE indicators in use Source: HEFCE (1999a)	Projected learning outcomes Research outputs	Non-completion rates Module completion rates	Research outputs/ staff costs Research outputs/ unit of funding Efficiency ratio: time students actually take to achieve an HE qualification divided by time that they should have taken	First destinations of graduates and leavers from HE. (HEFCE)

Efficiency	Output	Throughput	Internal efficiency	External efficiency
Proposed HE indicators Source: HEFCE (1999b)	Number achieving degree or other award Modules passed Publications/ citations Income from wholly or partially owned HE companies Value of industry research projects	% progressing at institution % transferring to another HEI % not progressing. % resuming studies % not resuming after two years	Cost per graduate Research share index: share of research costs per share of academic staff costs	% of graduates seeking employment Graduate destination indicators
School and college performance tables	Results by level of qualification Improvement measure: average A or A/S point score over the last four years	Number of students aged 16–18 Examination entries by level of qualification	DfEE statistics on participation in education and training by young people aged 16–18. (DfEE)	Youth Cohort Study (see Appendix 1.1)

Note: indicators shown in **bold** are currently in use or proposed; the others could be employed.

Gillborn and Youdell (2000) identify four ways of conceptualising educational equity:

1) *Formal equity*: where there are no explicit or formal barriers to participation on the basis of ascribed characteristics such as gender or ethnicity.

2) *Equality of circumstance*: where there are no economic barriers to prevent participation, such as prohibitive tuition fees.

3) *Equity of treatment*: where there is no discrimination involved in the process of education, such as the curriculum offered to students.

4) *Equity of outcomes*: where differences in achievement, employment and other benefits do not differ between groups on the basis of gender, ethnicity or social class.

It should be noted that performance indicators alone do not indicate whether or not structural barriers to access or progression in education exist. Patterns of participation or progression in education may also depend upon cultural factors and preferences. We can thus classify institutional performances in terms of equity:

1) Those related to conceptions of formal equity which record participation by gender or ethnicity;
2) Equality of circumstance indicators which relate to socio-economic status or disadvantage;
3) Equality of treatment indicators which relate to the progress of different groups in the education system;
4) Equality of outcome indicators which refer to differences in outcomes.

Table 3.2 indicates the range of equity performance criteria currently in use, or proposed for use, by a range of (but not necessarily all) lifelong learning providers. Again the distinction is drawn in the table between those currently in use or proposed and those that could be used.

Table 3.2 Current and proposed performance indicators for the equity of lifelong learning providers

Equity	Formal equity of access and provision	Equality of circumstance	Equity of treatment	Equity of outcome
FE indicators in use Source: FEFC (2000)	FE students disaggregated by ethnicity, gender and disability (FEFC)	FE students disaggregated by region, level of additional support required (FEFC)	Retention by ethnicity, gender and number of students who are eligible for the widening participation element (FEFC)	FE student destinations by ethnicity, gender and number of students who are eligible for the widening participation element (FEFC)
Proposed FE indicators Source: As above	As above	**% of students recruited by the College who are eligible for the widening participation funding element** **% of students who are eligible for the widening participation element and their relative level of deprivation**	As above	As above

Equity	Formal equity of access and provision	Equality of circumstance	Equity of treatment	Equity of outcome
HE indicators in use Source: HEFCE (1999a)	Students in HE – composition in terms of ethnicity and gender (HEFCE)	**% of students who attended a school or College in the state sector** **% of students whose parents occupation is 'skilled manual' 'semi-skilled' or 'unskilled'** **% who come from a neighbourhood (as denoted by its postcode) which is known to have a low proportion of 18–19-year-olds in education**	Higher education statistics for the United Kingdom includes data for progression disaggregated by affluence of neighbourhood, gender and ethnicity (HEFCE)	Higher education statistics for the United Kingdom includes data for destination disaggregated by affluence of neighbourhood, gender and ethnicity (HEFCE)
Proposed HE indicators Source: HEFCE (1999b)	As above	**Participation of young FT students from social classes III to IV** **Participation of young FT students from less affluent neighbourhoods** **Participation of young FT students from state school** **Participation of mature entrants with no previous HE qualifications** **Participation of mature entrants from less affluent neighbourhoods, with no previous HE qualifications**	**Progression from year of entry by affluence of neighbourhood** **Progression from year of entry for mature students entering with non-traditional qualifications**	**Qualifiers seeking employment from less affluent neighbourhoods** **Mature students seeking employment with non-traditional qualifications on entry**
School and College performance tables	**DfEE statistics on participation in education and training by young people aged 16–18 (DfEE)**	DfEE statistics on participation in education and training by young people aged 16–18 (DfEE)	DfEE statistics on participation in education and training by young people aged 16–18 (DfEE)	Youth Cohort Study (see Appendix 1.1)

Note: indicators in **bold** are currently in use or proposed; the others could be employed.

Table 3.2 shows that many of the performance indicators currently in use are concerned with equity of circumstance as measured by regional deprivation, social class, type of schooling or previous qualifications. There are no existing or proposed performance indicators that connect access or provision with ethnicity or gender (although some statistics are collected). Only in the HE sector have indicators relating equity of treatment to outcomes been proposed.

Qualification and policy aims

The final intermediate outcome of lifelong learning initiatives is the achievement of qualifications by individuals, post-16. Qualifications awarded form part of the stock of national qualifications, monitored as the National Education and Training Targets (NETTS). NETTS for 2002 are provided in Appendix 1.1.

Conclusion

Neither current, nor even proposed indicators, cover the full range of equity measures that are necessary to evaluate institutional performance. The assessment of equity of access and provision could be monitored through indicators based on ethnicity and gender. The assessment of equity of treatment and outcome becomes more problematic as the need to control for background characteristics becomes increasingly important.

We have identified areas where there are gaps concerning information on provider efficiency and equity. However, the introduction of additional performance indicators needs to be treated cautiously. For institutions, the recording and submission of additional information increases their administrative burden. The proliferation of performance indicators may also influence institutional behaviour in a manner unexpected by policy makers. For example, providers may lower quality standards in order to meet quantitative criteria (Leney et al., 1998).

MEASURING THE IMPACT OF LIFELONG LEARNING POLICIES

Figure 3.2 shows where selected individual lifelong learning initiatives could be expected to have an impact. The boxes in the diagram represent

Figure 3.2 Policy aims of key lifelong learning initiatives

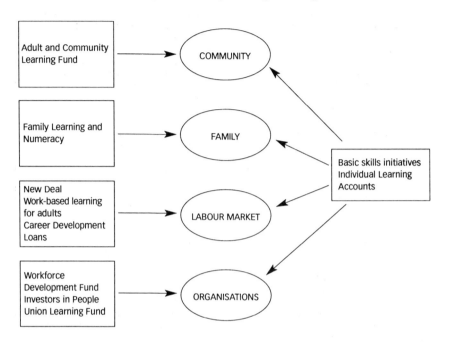

different lifelong learning policies organised by key area of impact (labour market, community, family and organisations). The arrows connect the policy measures with their key outcomes. For basic skills initiatives and Individual Learning Accounts, there is no single expected outcome of policy. It should be noted that in addition to the outcomes indicated, lifelong learning policies will be expected to have an impact on individual quality of life and the macro-economy as a whole.

Table 3.3 indicates the potential diversity of impacts of lifelong learning initiatives at the different levels of aggregation (McMahon, 1998). These are classified under two headings: non-monetary benefits to individuals and 'externalities' i.e. societal benefits. There have been various attempts within the UK and internationally to measure these impacts. We summarise and review the measures that have been used at the individual, family, community, organisational and macroeconomic level, using the idea of capital acquisition as a unifying theme.

Table 3.3 McMahon's outcomes for lifelong learning policies

Non-monetary benefits of lifelong learning	Externalities of lifelong learning
1. Health effects i) Reduced infant mortality ii) Lower illness rates iii) Greater longevity 2. Human capital produced in the home i) Children's education enhanced 3. More efficient household management i) Higher returns on financial assets ii) More efficient household purchasing 4. Labour force participation rates i) Higher female labour force participation rates ii) Reduced unemployment rates ii) More part-time employment after retirement 5. Lifelong adaption and continued learning i) Use of new technologies within the household (e.g. the Internet) ii) Obsolescence : human capital replacement investment iii) Curiosity and educational reading : educational T.V. / radio iv) Utilisation of adult education programmes 6. Motivational attributes i) Productivity of non-cognitive skills ii) Selective mating effects 7. Divorce and remarriage	1. Population and health effects i) Lower fertility rates ii) Lower net population growth rates iii) Public health 2. Democratisation i) Democratisation iii) Human rights ii) Political stability 3. Poverty reduction and crime i) Poverty reduction ii) Homicide rates iii) Property crime rates 4. Environmental effects i) Deforestation ii) Water pollution iii) Air pollution 5. Family structure and retirement i) Higher divorce rates ii) Later retirement iii) More work after retirement 6. Community service effects of education i) Time volunteered in community service within income strata ii) Generous financial giving within income strata iii) Knowledge dissemination through articles, books, television, radio, computer software and informally

Capital represents a stock of competences and dispositions. This overall stock can be broken down into stocks at different levels, essentially the same levels as those considered when assessing impact (Chapter 6). Human capital is a stock at the level of the individual learner whereas cultural capital is held by families. Identity capital includes elements related to human, cultural and social capital as well as specific psychological factors. It is a useful outcome in terms of individuals' ability to manage transitions. At a higher level of aggregation, intermediate or meso-economic forms of capital may be created within communities (social capital) and within and between organisations (intellectual capital).

Individual outcomes of lifelong learning

The labour market impacts of investment in human capital through lifelong learning are well known (Psacharapolous, 1995). The private rate of return to education provides policy makers with an indicator of employment and income benefits through education. This provides a measure of the worth of individuals' stock of human capital. Human capital is the accumulation of knowledge, skills and dispositions, which lead to labour market benefits (Schultz, 1961). In Chapter 6, we discuss methods by which the private rate of return to education in terms of such capital acquisition can be estimated.

Alternatively, other indicators of labour market success may be employed such as duration of unemployment (Payne, 1990) or 'work readiness' (DSS, 2000a, 2000b). In the UK, the Labour Force Survey (LFS) provides a number of indicators that have commonly been used in order to measure the effectiveness of lifelong learning initiatives. There may also be labour market outcomes for specific groups. McMahon (1998) gives an overview of key US research on labour market outcomes of lifelong learning such as part-time work after retirement and increased female labour force participation rates.

Apart from labour market benefits, individuals will experience increases in their quality of life through learning. Two key sources of quality of life indicators are the Human Development Index (United Nations, 1993) and the Index of Social Progress (Estes, 1998), although these measure aggregate, rather than individual, quality of life. More usefully, McMahon (1998) reviews key indicators of quality of life used in US studies on lifelong learning. These include utilisation of educational television and radio, lower illness rates and increased longevity of lifelong learners. In the UK, the birth cohort studies have been utilised to provide quality of life measures for learners. Bynner (1998) uses these data to report on impacts of learning on malaise (a mental health indicator) and individual resilience, amongst other outcomes.

Values and attitudes may be seen as a mediating variables as well as outcomes of lifelong learning (Schuller et al., 2000: 10–11). For example, changes in attitudes to community participation, to bringing up children and to lifestyle resulting from lifelong learning are key factors in influencing future behaviour. The British Social Attitudes survey and the General Household Survey are cross-sectional surveys which include scales for the assessment of values and attitudes.

Apart from human capital, it is also useful to consider investments in lifelong learning to increase individuals' stock of identity capital. Identity capital is a *set* of attributes comprising elements of human, cultural and social capital in addition to psychological constructs. Hence it spans individual (human), familial (cultural) and associational (social) forms of capital. Identity capital is defined as the collection of dispositions and behaviours which enable individuals to construct and reconstruct identities in order actively to manage transitions into and through adulthood (Côté, 1997). The tangible attributes of identity capital can include financial resources, educational credentials, socially rewarded competences and membership of clubs and associations. However, identity capital is more than a composite of other capital forms as it includes specific personality and attitudinal characteristics such as:

psychosocial vitalities and capacities such as the exploration of commitments, ego strength, an internal locus of control, self-monitoring, self-esteem, a sense of purpose in life, social perspective taking, critical thinking abilities and moral reasoning abilities. The common feature of these attributes is that they should give individuals the *wherewithal* to understand and negotiate the various social, occupational, and personal opportunities commonly encountered through (late-modern) life. (Côté, 1997: 578)

Family outcomes of lifelong learning

McMahon (1998) reviews studies of lifelong learning with family learning outcomes. A number of measurable indicators are included in these studies. Education effects on other family members may be measured by augmentation of the education of other individuals in the household. Angrist and Lavy (1996) show how these effects can be enumerated as savings to the exchequer (see p. 67). Additionally, McMahon (1998) identifies the use of new technologies within the home such as the internet and educational television as a measurable indicator of learning.

McMahon (1998) also identifies health and fertility indicators as lifelong learning outcomes. Lower fertility rates and delayed patterns of child bearing are associated with lifelong learning, as are improved levels of child health (Kenkel, 1991).

At the familial level, stocks of lifelong learning can be considered to form families' stock of cultural capital (Bourdieu and Passeron, 1990) i.e. the values, behaviours and dispositions (*habitus*) embraced by the middle classes and passed on from parents to children. Cultural capital underpins educational success, as educational institutions value middle- and upper-class values, dispositions and behaviour. Cultural capital is exchanged for educational credentials, which, in turn, are the key to economic success. Therefore, cultural capital is exchanged for economic capital via an apparently meritocratic route – the education system.

Community outcomes of lifelong learning

The concept of social capital has become important in enumerating community outcomes of learning. Social capital embraces features of social organisation such as networks of secondary associations, levels of trust and norms of mutual aid and reciprocity (Lochner et al., 1999).

Internationally, the World Bank has been instrumental in devising and utilising a number of research instruments to quantify social capital (Sudarsky, 1999). Lochner et al. (1999) provide a further review of available research instruments. Some progress has been made in the UK, mostly in the context of health. The Health Education Monitoring Survey (HEMS) has included questions on social capital since 1998. The British Household Panel Study introduced a social capital module to identify social capital at the local area level. There are similar plans for the new Millennium Cohort Study.

Aside from social capital, there a number of other measurable community outcomes from lifelong learning. Many local authorities already use indicators to measure community quality of life (DETR, 2000). These Central and Local Information Partnership (CLIP) indicators include:

- Households on benefits
- Participation rates in adult education
- Death rate by cause
- Unfit homes
- Homelessness
- Tenant satisfaction
- Community well-being
- Social participation
- Access to key services.

41

There is an ongoing consultation by the Audit Commission about the form and use of community indicators to extend CLIP. In particular, measures of crime and community safety are to be introduced.

Organisational outcomes of lifelong learning

In the UK, the Investors in People award (IIP) provides an indicator of the extent and effectiveness of in-house training and organisational learning. The number of firms gaining this award forms part of the NETTs. Local TECs also collect information about levels of information and training within firms.

Intellectual capital (or organisational intelligence) embraces the knowledge, skills, competences and abilities of an organisation. This includes the ability of organisations to accumulate further intellectual capital. It also refers to inter-organisational relationships. Westphalen (1999) provides a useful guide to the difficulties involved in recording organisational outcomes of learning, identifying it as an area where collaborative research is required.

Macro-economic outcomes of lifelong learning

In terms of the economy as a whole, learning may increase tax revenues through its impact on earnings and employment. The wider benefits of learning might also lead to a reduction in exchequer costs through improved health and intergenerational impacts (Bynner et al., 2001).

As a supply-side policy, learning increases the productivity and employability of individuals and the competitiveness of firms with beneficial consequences for economic growth. There may also be equity implications for income distribution, which will partly depend upon the distribution of human capital in the economy.

An example of modelling the impact of improvements on basic skills is provided in a recent WBL report (Bynner et al., 2001).

SUMMARY

Figure 3.3 provides an overall summary of the intermediate and final outcomes of lifelong learning policies as set out in previous sections. The bodies which comprise the learning infrastructure, and the partnerships and brokers involved in learning, are on the left-hand side of the diagram. In each box, we have listed the 'outcomes' of each of the bodies. As the LSC is the co-ordinating body in the sector, its outputs are dependent upon the performance of the sector as a whole. The next section of the diagram identifies various output measures for learning providers. Qualification and policy outcomes comprise the final 'intermediate outcome' of learning, i.e. the outcomes of specific policy initiatives in terms of the recruitment, retention and output of learners gaining qualifications. Final outcomes, in terms of impacts at various levels of aggregation, may be expected to vary from policy to policy (Figure 3.2). On the right-hand side of the diagram, we indicate that these outcomes may be quantified to estimate a full (rather than just labour market) private rate of return and a social rate of return to learning. These rates of return and methods of calculation will be discussed in Chapter 6.

As already discussed, there are a number of gaps in current knowledge concerning intermediate and final outcomes of UK lifelong learning. With reference to provider outcomes, indicators need to address efficiency and equity considerations.

Figure 3.3 **Intermediate and final outcomes of lifelong learning policies**

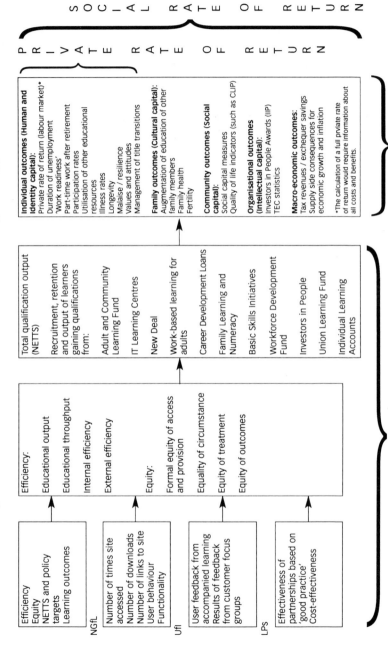

PRIVATE / SOCIAL

RATE OF RETURN

OF

RETURN

IMPACT

INTERMEDIATE OUTCOMES

Efficiency:
Educational output
Educational throughput
Internal efficiency
External efficiency

Equity:
Formal equity of access and provision
Equality of circumstance
Equity of treatment
Equity of outcomes

Total qualification output (NETTS)
Recruitment, retention and output of learners gaining qualifications from:
Adult and Community Learning Fund
IT Learning Centres
New Deal
Work-based learning for adults
Career Development Loans
Family Learning and Numeracy
Basic Skills Initiatives
Workforce Development Fund
Investors in People
Union Learning Fund
Individual Learning Accounts

Individual outcomes (Human and Identity capital):
Private rate of return (labour market)*
Duration of unemployment
'Work readiness'
Part-time work after retirement
Participation rates
Utilisation of other educational resources
Illness rates
Longevity
Malaise / resilience
Values and attitudes
Management of title transitions

Family outcomes (Cultural capital):
Augmentation of education of other family members
Family health
Fertility

Community outcomes (Social capital):
Social capital measures
Quality of life indicators (such as CLIP)

Organisational outcomes (Intellectual capital):
Investors in People Awards (IIP)
TEC statistics

Macro-economic outcomes:
Tax revenues / exchequer savings
Supply side consequences for economic growth and inflation

*The calculation of a full private rate of return would require information about all costs and benefits.

NGfL
Efficiency
Equity
NETTS and policy targets
Learning outcomes

Number of times site accessed
Number of downloads
Number of links to site
User behaviour
Functionality

Ufi
User feedback from accompanied learning
Results of feedback from customer focus groups

LPS
Effectiveness of partnerships based on 'good practice'
Cost-effectiveness

44

Chapter 4

Designs for Impact Evaluation

INTRODUCTION

Measuring the impact of a lifelong learning intervention is likely to be at the centre of most evaluation studies. By impact we mean the intervention's effects, both short term and long term, not only on the learners themselves, but also on their families, the communities in which they live and the organisations for whom they work. Was their position better than it would have been if there had been no intervention? Measuring impact raises a complex and difficult set of questions about research design. This chapter addresses the following major issues:

- Defining the target population for an intervention and its evaluation;
- Selecting control groups;
- Sampling.

    It also makes reference to publications that cover these issues in more detail than is possible in a report of this kind.

DEFINING THE TARGET POPULATION

There are two issues to consider when thinking about the target population for any intervention:

- What is the target population for the intervention?
- What is the target population for the evaluation?

The answers to these two questions might turn out to be identical but it is not necessary for this to be so. Decisions about the target population for the intervention are substantive ones, not amenable to a technical solution. The target population for the evaluation might, however, be based on technical and practical considerations as well as on substantive ones. For example, returning to the hypothetical education voucher intervention introduced in Chapter 2 (p. 16), the target population for the intervention could be all adults over 21 permanently resident in the LEAs, together with all those working for organisations with less than 100 employees located within the LEA boundaries. The target population for the impact evaluation might be restricted to LEA residents and employees in LEAs bordering the LEAs running the intervention. This restriction might be imposed to eliminate the substantial fieldwork costs that could be incurred collecting data from the minority of employees who travel long distances into work.

Another reason for differentiating between the two target populations is that we usually only want to estimate the impact of an intervention which has bedded down (although the process of bedding down is likely to be relevant in terms of understanding implementation). Consequently, the target population for an intervention such as a new basic skills programme in its first year of operation could reasonably be ignored for the evaluation of its impact. Most interventions will experience teething problems and it would not usually be desirable to allow these initial problems negatively to influence estimates of impact. Interventions based on extra financial input (vouchers, EMAs) could reasonably be assumed to bed down quickly but those based on new services or courses might take longer.

SELECTING CONTROLS

In order to attempt to establish a causal connection between an intervention and an outcome, some kind of control or comparison group is needed. Controls can be constructed in a number of ways. Here we consider the strengths and weaknesses of different approaches to collecting control data. We can divide these approaches into four broad groups:

1) methods that involve randomisation (or chance allocation) of individuals, or aggregates such as areas or institutions (or possibly both) to the intervention and control conditions;
2) methods that involve matching, either individuals or aggregates, so that one member of the matched pair receives the intervention, the other does not;
3) methods that involve comparisons with available (but self-selected and unmatched) controls;
4) methods that rely on comparisons with the past.

Selecting controls using randomisation

Randomisation is a powerful device which has, for many years, been the bedrock for experimental designs in medicine (clinical trials), agriculture (field trials) and psychology (laboratory experiments). Relying solely on chance to determine who does and does not receive an intervention is by far the best way of eliminating any systematic differences between intervention and control groups at the outset of an evaluation. Results from those social interventions that have used randomisation have usually been given more weight than those relying on methods involving a degree of self-selection. We note that the DfEE, in its tender document for the Collaborative Research Unit for Evidence Informed Policy and Practice has stated: 'we would wish to encourage greater use of randomly controlled trials in educational research'.

Any impact evaluation design that does not use some kind of randomisation in the way units are allocated to the intervention must involve a degree of self-selection. Hence, it will be subject to the problem that there could be systematic but unknown differences between the intervention and control groups. It is this problem which makes it difficult to assess the results from the Jarvis et al. (1997) evaluation of education vouchers described in Chapter 2. Vouchers were not assigned to a randomly selected subset of the target population and so it is difficult to separate any effects of the vouchers on outcomes from personal characteristics of those who chose to use them. Some of these selection differences, or choice mechanisms, can be 'controlled for' during the statistical analysis, some can be eliminated by careful matching in the design, although the opportunities for matching might be limited. However, neither of these methods can ever account completely for the fact that learners will select themselves into a programme for one or more reasons, and these reasons will not necessarily be transparent to the evaluator nor easily measured.

It is not always practicable randomly to assign individual learners to the intervention group. It might, however, be possible to introduce randomisation at an aggregate level. In other words, chance would determine which *areas* or which *institutions* received an intervention and which received the usual services. Cluster or group randomisation is often employed in health care research when, for example, different GP practices are assigned to treatment and control groups, and *all* patients in the treatment practices receive the intervention. In educational research it has been employed in the STAR experiment on class size (Word et al., 1990). An example from lifelong learning might involve randomly assigning a new kind of course to be delivered by some FE colleges and not others. The theory behind cluster randomisation is set out in Murray (1998).

We can illustrate how different kinds of randomisation could be implemented in a lifelong learning context by returning to the hypothetical educational vouchers intervention of Chapter 2. Within each LEA, vouchers could be allocated to a randomly selected subset of residents and employees, and the learning and other outcomes for this group could be compared with those not allocated a voucher. This would be better, from the point of view of a convincing evaluation, than just allowing potential learners to select themselves into the programme and comparing them with those not choosing to take up a voucher. It is, however, a design with one potential drawback. Allocating a voucher to someone who would not have chosen to have one could lead to a market in vouchers, with those not interested in a voucher offering to sell it to those interested but not allocated one. This problem of contamination (or diffusion or spillover or leakage) between intervention and control groups can change a randomised allocation to a self-selected one. One way of avoiding it in this situation would be first to establish who within the LEA would use a voucher if offered one and then randomly to allocate within that group of potential users. Indeed, this sub-population might be regarded as a more realistic target population than all residents and employees within the LEA but there could be practical difficulties in deciding who falls within it.

An alternative form of randomisation is to allocate a voucher scheme randomly to LEAs within the group of LEAs willing to administer it. This is an area randomisation that should prevent the formation of a market in vouchers if everyone in the LEA target population is offered one. A drawback of cluster randomised designs is that they are often lacking in statistical power, because the numbers of LEAs could be small. We shall return to this point below.

It would not be possible to escape from the problems of self-selection when comparing different monetary values of vouchers, if the LEAs themselves were free to determine its value, again because an LEA decision could be based on a number of unknown factors. The advantages of area randomisation would then be restricted to *overall* comparisons of voucher and non-voucher LEAs. On the other hand, it would be possible to maintain the advantages of randomisation if variation in the value of vouchers were built into the design at the outset and formed part of the randomisation. This could work if LEAs participating in the experiment (or pilot) were prepared to accept that they might not receive any extra resources in the form of vouchers and that they might have to accept a voucher of less value than another LEA.

Ethical considerations

The ethics of randomisation have received considerable attention in the literature, especially in medicine. In terms of the classification of interventions set out in Chapter 1, it is not possible to consider randomisation for the first three categories – provision available to anyone or at least to anyone who qualifies for it. It is, however, possible when demand exceeds supply so that an intervention can be rationed by chance (or lot). And it is, in principle, desirable when interventions are being tested by pilot projects. The weight of opinion in these situations favours the view that it is unethical *not* to randomise providing it is practicable to do so. This was expressed most strongly by Gilbert et al. (1975) who argue that not to randomise is 'fooling around with people'. Orr (1999) argues that, in situations where some kind of rationing is inevitable, then randomisation is fairer than relying on professional judgments about the perceived need for, and potential benefit from the intervention.

It would be desirable, when designing impact evaluations of lifelong interventions, to require that the case against randomisation should be presented. At the moment in educational and social research, and in marked contrast to medical and health care research, the case has to be made for it.

Matched controls

An alternative to randomisation is to try to select matched individuals or areas to serve as controls. This requires finding pairs of individuals or areas that are as similar as possible to one another, ideally differing only because one unit is getting the intervention and the other is not. Although matching is less powerful than randomisation, it is sometimes easier to implement.

The weakness of relying on matched controls is that units are in the intervention group for one or more reasons, and those reasons cannot necessarily be encapsulated by the set of indicators used to create matches. Consequently, comparisons between learners in, for example, voucher and non-voucher areas could be rendered invalid (biased) because of these unmeasured, and often unmeasurable, differences. In other words, we would not be comparing like with like, a problem that randomisation eliminates.

'Convenience' controls

The problem of self-selection is even more severe if the only controls available cannot even be matched, let alone randomised. In other words, the controls are non-users. In the absence of randomisation, it falls to statistical modelling to try to create the equivalent of a randomised design by introducing a set of statistical controls. We discuss these issues in more detail in Chapter 5.

Historical controls

Another way of creating controls is just to compare an outcome after the intervention with measures taken on one or more occasions before the intervention. We can represent this as follows:

(a)   O   X   O*
            or as:
(b)   O.......   O   X   O*.....O*

where O represents measures taken before the start of the intervention (baseline data or pre-tests), X represents the start of the intervention, and O* represents later measures (post-tests) which could be taken while the intervention is running and after it has finished.

Both these designs suffer from considerable disadvantages, the most important of which is not being able to separate change brought about by the intervention from change which would have happened anyway as a result of other societal changes. To use the language of Cook and Campbell (1979), these 'pretest-posttest' designs confound the possible effects of the intervention with the effects of 'history' and 'maturation'. Historical comparisons can be used to monitor change, as explained in Chapter 1, but they are of rather little value for evaluating impact. (Historical controls are transformed into convenience controls if a control group, not subject to the intervention, becomes available.)

SAMPLING

It is to be expected that a lifelong learning intervention could have effects at each of four levels: for the learner in terms of economic advantages and wider benefits such as improved health, for the learner's family in terms of increased support for learning for their children and other family members, for the learner's community in terms of, say, greater civic participation and for the learner's work organisation in terms of increased productivity. If effects for each of these levels are postulated, then it follows that each must be sampled in order to measure them.

In addition, it is likely that many interventions will be heterogeneous both in the way in which they are delivered and in the way they are experienced by learners. This heterogeneity needs to be represented in the evaluation design. Sometimes the heterogeneity is planned, as it could be in the vouchers example with levels of financial support varying from LEA to LEA. Quite often, the heterogeneity arises because interventions are delivered by people within organisations, and these people will differ in their enthusiasm for the programme, in their ability to deliver it, and so on. Moreover, some interventions will be experienced in different ways by different members of the target population, even if they are delivered uniformly. For example, an intervention aimed at improving computer awareness in the workplace might be experienced differently by men and women.

Areas, institutions and organisations

The inherent heterogeneity of many interventions, together with variety in context, creates some problems for the design of an impact evaluation. But it also creates considerable opportunities for understanding a range of effects that a more uniform intervention would not create. We can, for example, consider if the effect of an intervention such as a voucher is modified according to whether the scheme is administered by the LEA or by a local college, or by the enthusiasm of the employer. These kinds of aggregate effects are potentially important but they can only be measured precisely if a reasonably sized sample of these aggregates is included. We return to this point below but note that, often, the optimum sampling strategy will be to include all the aggregates, and a similar number of controls, in the sample.

Families and children

The sample of families will usually be defined by the selected sample of learners. Although there is often an argument for including all aggregates in the sample, it is not always so important to include a large number of learners per area. It is, however, important to have a sample of sufficient size to be able to analyse the impact of the intervention on sub-groups, for example, ethnic and other minorities.

Occasions

If a longitudinal design is chosen, consideration must be given to the number and timing of the measurement occasions. If allowance for selection effects has to be made through statistical analysis then it is particularly important to obtain measurements on all relevant variables *before* the intervention starts. Thus, if a longitudinal design is chosen, consideration must be given to the number and timing of the measurement occasions.

It will also be important to recognise that there will be attrition from a longitudinal sample as a result of refusals and later drop-out of learners. It is possible that refusals and attrition in any control areas will be greater than in the intervention areas. This will have implications for the size of the target sample.

Sample Size

The question of sample size is strongly related to the issue of statistical power. It is important to have a sample that is sufficiently large to pick up differences of substantive interest in the population. If the sample is too small, then genuine differences of interest are swamped by sampling error. Power calculations are somewhat more complicated for designs with clustering, as explained by Murray (1998). We have to allow for the fact that people living close to one another in the same area, or working for the same firm, or attending the same course, tend to be more similar on average than people living in different areas or working for different firms and so on. Moreover, any impact evaluation will, because of the multi-faceted nature of many interventions, perforce be concerned with a range of outcomes. Nevertheless, it is possible to get some indication of the sample size required for different percentage changes from different baselines, under different degrees of similarity within clusters. An example of varying levels of power for different designs is given in the report on the Sure Start Evaluation Development Project (JCLR, 2000).

CONCLUSION

This chapter has covered the major design issues involved in estimating the size of the intervention on the target population. It emphasises the importance of controls and explains how these controls might be obtained. Randomisation is the ideal here but it is not always practicable. The likelihood that an intervention will be designed to have effects at more than one level – on families, communities and employing organisations – as well on individual learners, has implications for sampling and statistical analysis that are considered in more detail in the next chapter. Analyses that estimate links between implementation and impact – the analysis of process – are also important.

Figure 4.1 sets out these issues as a series of steps and shows how different ways of selecting controls come together again when sampling is being considered, and how samples at different levels are brought together by statistical analysis.

Figure 4.1 Design stages for estimating impact

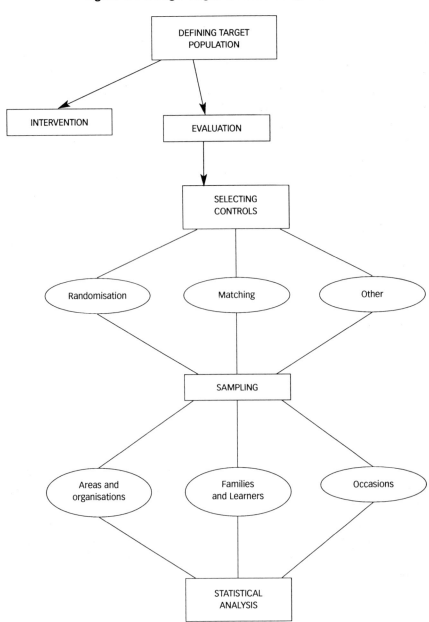

Chapter 5

Estimating Impact using Statistical Modelling

INTRODUCTION

As we have already pointed out, there are considerable obstacles in the way of estimating the impact of an intervention when there are no designed controls that have been generated by randomisation (ideally), or by matching. In these situations, the emphasis shifts away from issues of research design towards methods of statistical analysis. This is not to suggest that design becomes irrelevant because questions about sampling, in particular, are still important. Nevertheless, the analysis of a well-designed randomised experiment is relatively straightforward whereas an appropriate analysis of an uncontrolled or observational study can be a difficult and time-consuming task. This chapter sets out the broad issues that need to be addressed when estimating the effect of an intervention using observational or survey data and concludes with some thoughts about statistical analysis.

FUNDAMENTAL ISSUES

Suppose we wish to estimate the effect of attending UfI. Do UfI **learndirect** learners have higher incomes, better health and so on than those not attending? (We use UfI as a peg on which to hang these issues but, of course, there are a number of other interventions with essentially the same characteristics for evaluation, as set out in Chapter 1.)

A simple-minded approach to this question would be, first, to sample **learndirect** learners and, separately, non-users; second, to estimate means for the two groups (mean income, say); and finally to calculate a mean difference:

$$D = \bar{y}_u - \bar{y}_{nu},$$ where subscripts 'u' and 'nu' refer to users and non-users.

If this difference were positive then one might conclude that UfI has a positive effect on incomes, if zero (or even negative) then UfI has no effect on future income. Such conclusions are, however, very likely to be mistaken. Or, to put it more precisely, the mean difference, D, will be a biased estimator of the effect of the intervention, bearing in mind that what we really want to know is what would have happened to the incomes of those attending UfI if they had not actually attended, or, equivalently, what would have happened to those not attending had they, in fact, been UfI students.

Under what circumstances will D be a biased estimator of the intervention effect? It will happen if there are variables – often known as 'confounding' variables – that are correlated with income *and* are also correlated with use of UfI. It is not difficult to think of candidates for membership of this group of variables. It is, for example, possible that more men than women learn with UfI. Given that men's incomes tend to be higher than women's anyway, a positive value of D might just reflect this gender imbalance rather than an effect of the intervention. In other words, both income and use of UfI are correlated with gender. The same kinds of arguments could be applied to ethnic variables and to age.

There is another group of confounding variables that pose particular problems. These are variables like 'motivation' and 'ambition' that are difficult to measure and which are at the heart of the problem of self-selection referred to previously (p. 6). People select themselves into interventions like UfI because they are, for example, more motivated than their peers, and these differences in motivation are generally found even after more easily measured variables such as age and social background have been allowed for. Consequently, it is crucial to collect as much information as possible about those variables which (a) determine *why* learners choose to select themselves into, or out of, an intervention, and (b) are correlated with the outcomes of interest.

EMBEDDING CONTROL INTO THE RESEARCH DESIGN

There are two ways of trying to deal with the problem of self-selection. Ideally, they should be used in combination. The first is to design the evaluation so that some of the problems are eliminated at this stage (Kish, 1987). The second, and generally more important way is to deal with the problem in the analysis.

Dealing first with design, it would not, for example usually be sensible to compare **learndirect** learners with a random sample from the non-UfI population because the latter will include Higher Education graduates who would be expected to have higher incomes. Hence, HE graduates would need to be screened out in some way at the design stage. In essence, this is just the issue discussed in Chapter 4 about defining the target population.

Second, it would be possible to restrict the evaluation to looking at the effect of UfI just on men's incomes, say, and so avoiding the problem of a gender imbalance in the user and non-user groups. This would, of course, also restrict the generalisability of any findings but could be a sensible strategy if a substantial majority of **learndirect** learners were men. It would even be possible to restrict the samples to men in a certain age group, say 30–34. If estimated effects for both men and women were required then it would be important to stratify the sample in such a way to ensure that both sexes were adequately represented in the user and non-user samples.

The third design issue is perhaps the most important. It is well established in many areas of quantitative social science that the best predictor of the future course of a variable is the current value of that variable. So, future incomes of **learndirect** learners and their non-UfI peers will be strongly correlated with their incomes *before* they start on a UfI programme. Hence, we always need a pre-intervention (or pre-test) measure of the outcome. This, in turn, implies that, even for measuring short-term outcomes, a longitudinal design is needed.

CREATING CONTROL IN THE ANALYSIS

There is a vast statistical literature on methods for drawing causal inferences from observational data and it would not be appropriate to go into
detail here. Instead, we signpost the variety of techniques. Most of these
techniques are based, to a greater or lesser degree, on multiple regression
models for longitudinal data.

Suppose we have two groups (UfI and non-UfI), and, for each sample
member, measures of income before learners started with UfI and equivalent measures at an appropriate interval after finishing. We could then set
up the following simple statistical model:

$$y_i = b_0 + b_1 x_i + b_2 d_i + e_i \quad (5.1)$$

where y_i is the measure of income for individual i after the intervention (the
post-test), x_i is the pre-intervention measure of income, d_i is a variable taking
the value 0 for non-users and 1 for users and e is the usual error term. Our
interest is in the estimate of b_2, the coefficient for the group variable. If it is
positive, *and if the specification of the model is correct*, then there is evidence
that UfI raises incomes because the interpretation of b_2 is that, for fixed
levels of income before the intervention is experienced, users have higher
incomes later.

The key issue for the approach represented by model (5.1) is whether the
model is a complete specification of both the selection and outcome
processes. In other words, do variations in income between the two groups
before entering UfI account for all the self-selection, and is the same linear
relation between the two measures of income appropriate for both groups?
The answer to the first question is likely to be 'no'. As we have already noted,
variables such as motivation are likely to influence participation in UfI and
are likely to influence future income over and above levels of current
income. Hence, other control variables need to be incorporated into model
(5.1). These issues are discussed in some detail in Plewis (1985, Ch. 3).

A second statistical approach is to use a 'difference of differences' estimator. In its simplest form, this just means calculating:

$$\left(\bar{y}_1 - \bar{y}_0 \right) - \left(\bar{x}_1 - \bar{x}_0 \right) \quad (5.2)$$

where $\bar{y}_1$ and $\bar{y}_0$ are the post-intervention mean incomes, for the intervention and control groups, and $\bar{x}_1$ and $\bar{x}_0$ are the corresponding pre-intervention means. This estimator will eliminate fixed unobserved differences between the two groups but at a cost of a number of assumptions. It also suffers from the disadvantage that differences are not always easily interpretable, especially when the variables are not measured on a fixed scale. Consequently, the estimator might work well for income but not for a measure of health. Further details about estimators like (5.2), which tend to be favoured by economists, can be found in Heckman and Hotz (1989).

A third approach is to use 'propensity score' matching as described by, for example, Rosenbaum and Rubin (1983). This approach first models the selection process and, based on an estimate of the probability that someone in the sample will choose to participate in the intervention, incorporates this selection process into the process for the outcome. This approach is similar to the 'instrumental variables' approach often used in econometrics.

Other useful references to methods for modelling the impact of evaluations with observational data are Anderson et al. (1980) and Heckman and Singer (1985).

MODELLING OUTCOMES AT DIFFERENT LEVELS

As we pointed out in Chapter 4, we are not only interested in outcomes at the level of the individual learner but also in outcomes for the learner's family, their community and the organisation for which they work. For example, we might expect participation in UfI to raise learners' incomes and also to increase their involvement in their children's education and to improve the efficiency of their work environment.

An impact evaluation design that is concerned with estimating effects at different levels is likely to generate a large and complex dataset, requiring the application of a number of modern, computer-intensive statistical techniques for longitudinal and multilevel data. One possible structure would have the following multilevel, or hierarchical, or nested, form:

AREA/COMMUNITY/ORGANISATION LEVEL FOUR
FAMILY LEVEL THREE
LEARNER LEVEL TWO
MEASUREMENT OCCASION LEVEL ONE

In other words, families are nested in areas and organisations, learners are nested in families, and the repeated measures generated by a longitudinal design – the measurement occasions – are nested within learners. This structure assumes that there is more than one learner per family in at least some families. There would be a number of measures at level four such as whether it is an urban or rural area, whether it is an organisation in the public or private sector and, in a cluster randomised design (see p. 48), whether the area is an intervention or a control area. Some of the family and learner measures will be constant – social class and gender, for example, but others – family functioning, for example – could vary across occasions. A more complicated structure is generated if both areas and employing organisations are included in the sample. This is because learners will, in general, be cross-classified by area of residence and employing organisation. Multilevel models for cross-classified structures are discussed by Goldstein (1995).

Methods for multilevel analysis for these kinds of data structures are set out in Plewis (1997) and, in an evaluation context, in Plewis and Hurry (1998) and Plewis (2000a). Plewis (2000b) focuses particularly on the issue of modelling impact heterogeneity. It is well known that the value and power of these methods is very much greater when there is a reasonably large sample of units at the highest level, in this case areas or organisations. This is another reason for including all areas or institutions in the sample.

It is worth stressing that it is only possible to use models of this kind with data measured at the lowest level of aggregation. Indeed, it is, in general, extremely difficult to estimate the impact of an intervention on individual learners, and different kinds of learners, without data collected on those learners. Aggregate data are very likely to be misleading.

Another important part of any analysis will be to model effects on the outcomes in terms of the linkages generated by the implementation side of the evaluation, and the theories of change, as discussed in Chapter 2. If the intervention works, why does it work (and for whom and in which contexts)? Statistical tools such as regression models for change of the kind discussed above (p. 58) and structural equations models will be applicable here. It must also be remembered that some of the outcomes are likely to be binary or categorical and will need to be analysed with more specialised techniques – logistic regression and log-linear models, for example – than multiple regression. In the same way, the wider benefits of an intervention that has an impact on learning will need to be modelled and this is especially so for estimating rates of return in a cost-benefit analysis, as we show in Chapter 6.

CONCLUSION

This chapter has outlined how to tackle the thorny issue of estimating effects for an intervention where there is a considerable amount of self-selection. These issues can be dealt with partially at the design stage with a clear definition of the target population and a careful sampling scheme, together with extensive measurement of all possible confounding variables. Longitudinal designs will nearly always be needed. Statistical analysis will always be a crucial weapon in the fight against the many ruses of self-selection and reference is made to a variety of techniques.

Figure 5.1 sets out the steps involved in modelling impacts at different levels. These levels appear at a number of stages – during sampling (as discussed in Chapter 4), measurement and analysis.

Figure 5.1 Steps in modelling Impact

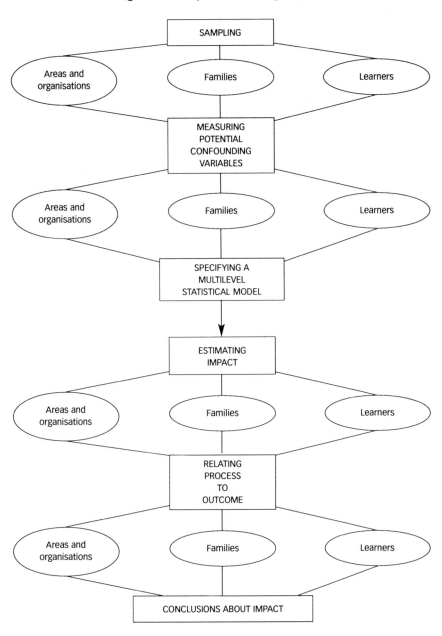

Chapter 6

Cost-Benefit Analysis (CBA)

INTRODUCTION

From the perspectives of government, institutional providers of lifelong learning, and ultimately the taxpayer, a crucial aspect of evaluation is the relationship between the economic benefits of learning and its costs. The assessment in monetary terms of the costs and benefits of a project can enable the above parties to assess the efficiency of their actions against alternatives.

The validity of CBA (Cost-Benefit Analysis) depends upon the adequacy of the impact evaluation discussed in Chapter 4. The conversion of private benefits (those which accrue to the individual) and external benefits (those which accrue to society) into monetary values will be based upon the statistical estimates calculated at this stage. It is assumed, in conducting a CBA of an intervention to increase learning, that there is an established causal link between the intervention, learning, and its associated benefits and costs.

A CBA of a lifelong learning intervention would be conducted in four stages. First the impact evaluation would estimate a set of effects between a policy intervention on the one hand (such as a voucher scheme) and learning outcomes (such as obtaining a qualification) on the other. Next, the impact of the learning outcome on related benefits of learning (such as increased income, employment opportunities, better health or reduced crime) would be assessed. In the third stage of the CBA these benefits would be transformed into a stream of monetary values over time. Finally, these would be combined with educational costs and expressed as a percentage rate of return to education, a monetary net present value, or both. These valuations could then be compared with alternative investment opportunities so as to make a judgement about the efficiency of expenditure. In this chapter we will concern ourselves with the stages which would follow an impact evaluation.

BENEFITS OF LEARNING

As discussed in Chapter 3, we can expect that there will be both individual (private) and social (external) benefits arising from learning. For the individual, the private benefits of learning are in terms of increased income and a reduced probability of unemployment. In addition to raising the general level of income at each age, investment in education also means that earnings rise at an increased rate and peak at a later stage than for those individuals with a lower level of education. The individual and their family will also experience some of the wider benefits of education such as improved health, intergenerational impacts and expanding social networks.

The external benefits of education for the exchequer will arise from increases in income tax and national insurance. Due to improved employment opportunities, individuals will be less likely to depend upon state benefits. Other external benefits of education may include savings to the National Health Service through improvements in individual health, together with reductions in crime and increases in the rate of economic growth.

ASCRIBING MONETARY VALUES TO THE BENEFITS OF EDUCATION

A number of techniques could be employed to value the employment and income related (private) benefits from education but the wider benefits of education – with the exception of taxation and welfare benefit savings –

have not conventionally been included in CBA. However, work is emerging in this area of the economics of education and Wolfe and Zuvekas (1997), in addition to McMahon (1997, 1998), provide an overview of evaluation methods which may be employed to measure the wider benefits of learning. We will provide an overview of how, given a statistical relationship between learning and its benefits, monetary values could be placed on major private and external benefits. In each case we will explain how we could assess the monetary value of each impact on an individual. Individual data would then be aggregated to include all individuals experiencing the learning and either discounted back to the present or used to calculate a rate of return (see 'Methods of calculation', below for an explanation of these techniques).

Employment and income (private) benefits

By using a Mincerean earnings function (Mincer, 1974), a statistical relationship between net earnings on the one hand, and education and other socio-economic variables on the other, could be constructed. In this manner, the impact of learning between those individuals who did and did not participate in the learning intervention could be established across life cycles.

The Mincerean earnings function is essentially a regression model:

$$\text{Log } w = \beta_0 + \beta_1 S + \beta_2 X + \beta_3 X^2 + \beta_4 Z + \varepsilon \qquad (6.1)$$

In the above equation, w represents earnings, S number of years of schooling – the education variable of interest, X years of labour market experience and Z 'other' variables. The parameters β_i (i = 0...4) are to be estimated and ε is an error term.

If the log of earnings is used as a dependent variable, then the effect of education on earnings can be read off as the estimate of β_1 for each year of labour market experience. It is standard practice to specify separate earnings functions by gender. Variables specifying employment sector (Grootaert, 1990) and family background (Bennett et al., 1995) may also be included in the earnings function. When combined with the impact of education on the probability of employment, a monetary value can be ascribed to this private benefit.

Let us assume that without a learning intervention, such as the voucher scheme discussed on p. 16, an individual with a number of years of labour market experience would earn an annual wage w^0 and have an employment probability of 86 per cent. From the Mincerean earnings function it is possible to estimate the effect of additional years of schooling (S) on earnings. In our example, we will assume that the extra years of education associated with lifelong learning have increased wages above what they would otherwise be by 10 per cent. In addition, we will assume that the probability of employment is increased by 5 per cent due to the intervention. Therefore, expected earnings with the intervention will be:

$$Y^1 = w^0 (0.86 + 0.05) (1+0.1)$$

Without the intervention, expected earnings would be:

$$Y^0 = 0.86w^0$$

The percentage increase in gross earnings is $(Y^1 - Y^0) / Y^0$. As

$$Y^1-Y^0 = w^0(0.86+0.05)(1+0.1) - 0.86 \ w^0$$

the percentage increase is therefore:

$$((0.91*1.1) - 0.86) / 0.86 = 0.1639$$

This implies that the intervention increases earnings by 16.4 per cent. If earnings of individuals with a fixed level of labour market experience were £15,000 p.a., each individual will earn £2,458.50 more in this year as a result of the intervention. Using the Mincerean earnings function and knowledge of employment probabilities from the impact evaluation, the procedure could be repeated for each year of the life-cycle.

One disadvantage with the above procedure is the requirement for panel data collected over the life-cycle. To estimate the impact on earnings and employment within a shorter time frame, employment and earnings data for a few years following the intervention could be extrapolated with the attendant risks involved in such extrapolation. Alternatively, the earnings and employment probability differentials which persist in these early years may be taken to be a proxy of those in subsequent ones to enable a 'short-cut' calculation of the benefits to be made (Psacharapolous, 1995).

If gross earnings are used in the Mincerean earnings function (model 6.1), then increases in income tax and national insurance could be calculated although it would be more difficult to calculate welfare benefit savings without knowledge of other elements of the individual's life-history such as family structure. Alternatively, existing simulation models such as the Institute of Fiscal Studies tax and benefit model TAXBEN could be used to provide an indication of such savings.

Wider benefits (private and external)

Other benefits of education, such as potential impacts on health, crime and families, are both private and external as they affect both individuals and society – most obviously in terms of savings to the exchequer. We illustrate how it may be possible to assess the impact of learning for the family and for society with reference to two examples.

Let us first take the case of a private health benefit arising from education. We will assume that a research finding shows that education increases longevity by 0.1 years for each additional year spent in education beyond 16. We would then attempt to estimate the cost of producing the outcome of increased longevity by alternative means, perhaps through the purchase of health care inputs. This is assumed to be the value that the individual would place on their improved longevity.

Angrist and Lavy (1996) provide an actual example of an intergenerational impact of learning to illustrate the possible valuation of external benefit for an individual, although a similar procedure could be used to evaluate other non-monetary benefits of education. The study provides estimates of the impact of a mother's education on the number of times a child repeats a grade at school. They find that an additional dollar of household income reduces the odds that a child will repeat a grade by 0.002. Additionally, a mother's high school diploma reduces the odds that a child will repeat a grade by 0.620. So the private benefit (P_b) is:

$$P_b = (0.620 / 0.002) * \$1 = \$310$$

Therefore the mother's high school diploma is equivalent to an additional $310 of household income and so the 'value' of this private benefit (P_b) for the household could be assumed to be the same. Alternatively, the cost of achieving the same increase in the child's ability through privately purchased educational services such as home tuition could be used. In addition to the private benefits, there will also be wider external benefits in terms of savings on educational expenditure and these could also be factored into the analysis.

In the case of an external benefit for the community a similar approach could be used. For example, let us assume that a research finding indicates that each year of education reduces the probability that someone commits a criminal offence by 0.5 per cent after controlling for other factors. There are two ways in which the monetary cost to the government could be measured. First, the cost to the government of achieving a similar reduction in the crime rate by other means could be input as a 'shadow price'. Second, the benefit to society from the savings made in terms of the judicial system and costs of imprisonment could be calculated.

Effects can also be measured at the community level in an aggregated form (McMahon, 1998: 326). If relationships between poverty reduction and education, and crime and poverty reduction could be assessed then a relationship between education and crime can be established. For example, if a year's learning leads to a £1,000 increase in income per year and if a £1,000 increase in income leads to a 0.5 per cent reduction in crime then the impact of a year's education on crime is also 0.5 per cent.

NACRO's (1998) report, *Wasted Lives*, attempts to quantify the costs of youth crime with reference to earlier Home Office and private sector studies on this topic. The basis for the cost analysis is a non-random sample of 45 respondents held in three institutions. The average cost of crimes committed to date, criminal justice response costs and family intervention and care costs are estimated to be £75,365 for each respondent. Note that the figure of £75,365 does not include the effects of crime on individual's and other's health, nor does it take into account possible cumulative effects of crime in terms of the probability of re-offending. If an impact evaluation assessed that the result of a specific educational project for young offenders were to reduce the probability of ever offending by 1 per cent then the external benefit (E_b) of this project to society for each potential offender would be:

$$E_b = £75,365*0.01 = £753:65$$

One final significant external benefit of learning is the impact on the general level of economic growth. As in the case of the impact of learning on taxes and benefits, the use of econometric modelling would be necessary in order to arrive at any robust conclusions. Without such modelling, the general increase in wages could be taken to be a proxy for output as in Bynner et al. (2001). However, this approach makes a number of assumptions regarding the relationship between wages and productivity and the future share of wages as a proportion of Gross Domestic Product (GDP). In addition, recent developments in economic growth modelling allow for the endogeneity of human capital investment, with investments in education and health resulting from, and also, being an input to, growth (McMahon, 1998).

COSTS OF LEARNING

The direct costs of a lifelong learning intervention for the government will include the costs of implementation, administration and evaluation. It may be difficult in some cases to allocate direct costs to separate programmes, in particular when one provider is responsible for a range of education or training. The direct costs of lifelong learning may sometimes be shared between the government and the individual recipient in terms of tuition fees.

The primary indirect private cost of lifelong learning is the possible loss of individual earnings, and hence tax revenues, whilst the individual is involved in learning. This would apply primarily to full-time education. In addition, there may be less explicit external costs such as 'qualification inflation' or over-education which are usually not included in CBA. Groot and Van Den Brink (1997) use the BHPS to estimate the external costs of over-education in the United Kingdom and a similar method could, in principle, be followed in a future evaluation.

METHODS OF CALCULATION

Costs and benefits arising from lifelong learning will accrue throughout the lifecycle. Some, such as fees and foregone earnings will fall relatively soon after the decision to enter learning. Others, such as health benefits, will be felt later in life, and intergenerational benefits by succeeding cohorts. Due to inflation and the time preferences of individuals and governments, revenue streams in the future are worth less than those in the present. These future streams of benefits and costs should therefore be discounted to reflect this and there are two ways in which the procedure of discounting may be conducted. The Net Present Value method of calculation inputs a discount rate into the CBA. The alternative, the Internal Rate of Return, is the discount rate at which the expected stream of benefits is equal to the expected stream of costs. Although there are obvious similarities between the two methods, each has its particular advantages and disadvantages.

In each case, it would be possible to calculate a private return or value of learning where the costs and benefits used are those which accrue to the individual, or a social return or value of learning where all costs and benefits – both private and external – are included. The calculation of private and social rates is illustrated in the example on p. 72.

The Net Present Value (NPV) method

The NPV is the value of the discounted benefits of learning, minus the discounted value of its costs. The formula for the NPV is:

$$NPV = \sum_{t=0}^{n} \frac{(B_t - C_t)}{(1 + r)^t}$$

where B_t and C_t represent benefits and costs at time t, n is the time at which the stream of benefits and costs arising from the learning end, r is the discount rate and NPV is the Net Present Value.

The Internal Rate of Return (IRR) method

The IRR (r^*) is the rate of discount at which the benefits and costs of learning are equalised over an individual's life, obtained by solving:

$$\sum_{t=0}^{n} \frac{(B_t - C_t)}{(1 + r^*)^t} = 0$$

where B_t and C_t represent benefits and costs at time t, n is the time at which the stream of benefits and costs arising from the learning end and r^* is the internal rate of return.

Each method of calculation has its own advantages and disadvantages. The Internal Rate of Return is the predominant method utilized in the literature (Asplund and Pereira, 1999 provide a survey of European results in this form), by the Organisation for Economic Co-operation and Development (OECD,1996, 1997, 1998), and the World Bank. So this method of calculation is attractive in terms of making comparisons between returns to lifelong learning and existing returns to other forms of education. In addition, it does not require the input of a discount rate. However, for evaluation purposes the Net Present Value method may be preferable for two reasons. First, the discount rate of 6 per cent as set by the Treasury in the Green Book for investments in fixed capital is the usual benchmark on which government projects are assessed. Second, in unusual situations where the costs and benefits of education do not follow a standard pattern, a unique solution for the Internal Rate of Return may not be attained.

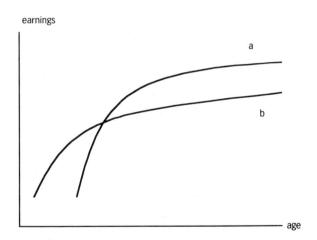

In the diagram (above), the two Mincerean earnings functions represent the typical relationship between age and earnings (age-earnings profiles) for two otherwise similar individuals who have experienced differing levels of education with 'a' obtaining relatively more education than 'b'. The benefits of education for 'a' are realised at the point where the earnings functions cross. In this typical situation it is possible to calculate both the IRR and the NPV.

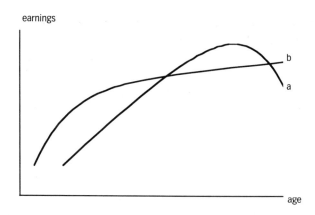

The second diagram shows an atypical relationship between age and earnings for individual 'a' whose earnings function unusually declines with age. This could be due to a rapid depreciation of 'a's skills. In this situation, the age-earnings profiles of 'a' and 'b' cross twice and calculation of the IRR would not result in a unique solution. In this, admittedly rare situation, only the calculation of the NPV would be meaningful.

Clearly, both the NPV and the IRR can be calculated for the majority of educational expenditures, with the NPV being suitable for departmental use where the Green Book discount rate of 6 per cent is of central importance, and the IRR being employed in cases where comparisons are made with results from the academic literature.

CASE STUDY: COST-BENEFIT ANALYSIS OF THE VOUCHER SCHEME

We will continue with our example of the voucher scheme from earlier chapters in order to show how a CBA calculation could be performed and how an assessment could be made about the efficiency of the scheme. We will calculate figures to show both the individual (private) returns and valuations alongside the social return. Sensitivity analysis is used to indicate how these values might be expected to change under differing assumptions.

In this example, let us initially assume that the LEA requires the individual to make a contribution of £200 towards their voucher. For simplicity we will assume that learning can be carried out whilst the individual remains in employment. This means that there is no need to include forgone earnings as a private cost.

Individual benefits would be both monetary and non-monetary. The effects of learning on these benefits would have been ascertained as described in pp. 64–9. In the following example, benefits from an increased probability of employment and increased earnings will be £20, up to the retirement age of 65. We will assume that individuals receive benefits in terms of reduced health expenditure equivalent to £5 per year.

Let us assume that this LEA will provide a voucher with a face value of £600. As the student has contributed £200 towards the voucher cost, the external cost to the LEA is £400. For the purpose of this example, we will not include administration and other related costs of provision.

External benefits would be in terms of increased tax revenue, taken to be £2 in this example and possible savings in areas such as health and crime (assumed to be £20). Again, non-monetary benefits can be accounted for by using the methods described earlier in this chapter. Other benefits, such as social cohesion, may be more difficult to express in monetary terms.

Once the pattern of costs and benefits through the individual's life cycle has been established, rates of return and present values could be calculated using the formulae provided above. Table 6.1 gives the results of such a calculation. Let us assume that the individual in this case was aged 25 when they used the voucher to purchase an adult education course and will live to age 70. The private cost of use is £200. When controlling for other variables, the additional education adds £20 each year in earnings and, in addition, leads to a private health benefit of £5 each year. The private net benefits row yields a private rate of return of 12 per cent and has a Net Present Value to the individual of £168.12.

Now let us factor in the external benefits and costs of voucher use. For the LEA costs of £400 will be incurred. External benefits are the increased tax revenue through earnings and reduction in crime and health costs. The net social benefits row is the sum of the net private benefits and the external costs (voucher cost to the LEA) and external benefits (tax revenue, crime and health benefits) of the project. The net social benefits row of Table 6.1 yields a social rate of return of 7 per cent and a net present value of £110.77. If we assume that 10,000 individuals participate in the voucher scheme then the total (social) Net Present Value would be £1.1077 million. The social rate of return, or Net Present Value, or both could then be compared to alternative projects.

Table 6.1 Outcomes of the voucher scheme

Age	25	26–65	66–70	IRR	NPV
Voucher Cost	−200	0	0		
Increased Earnings	0	20	0		
Health Benefits	0	5	5		
Net Private Benefit	−200	25	5	12%	£168.12
Voucher Cost	−400	0	0		
Tax Revenue	0	2	0		
Reduced Crime / Health Costs	0	20	20		
Net Social Benefit	−600	47	25	7%	£110.77

Let us now change one of the original outcomes of the voucher scheme described above to illustrate the sensitivity of the IRR and NPV to changes in costs and benefits close to the *start* of an intervention. If the cost of the voucher to the individual and the Local Authority were halved but the resulting benefits remained the same, then the private and social benefits of the project would increase dramatically.

Table 6.2 A reduction in costs of the voucher for both individuals and society

Age	25	26–65	66–70	IRR	NPV
Voucher Cost	−100	0	0		
Increased Earnings	0	20	0		
Health Benefits	0	5	5		
Net Private Benefit	−100	25	5	25%	£262.46
Voucher Cost	−200	0	0		
Tax Revenue	0	2	0		
Reduced Crime / Health Costs	0	20	20		
Net Social Benefit	−300	47	25	16%	£393.79

Compared with Table 6.1, Table 6.2 shows that the private IRR has increased from 12 per cent to 25 per cent and the social IRR from 7 per cent to 16 per cent. The private NPV has increased from £168.12 to £262.46 and the social NPV from £110.77 to £393.79.

Similarly, it can be shown that changes in costs and benefits later in the individual's life-cycle would make little significant difference to the returns. For example, if the private health related benefits from education after 65 increase from £5 to £100 this makes little difference to the IRR when compared with Table 6.1.

Table 6.3 Increase in private health benefits arising after the age of 65

Age	25	26–65	66–70	IRR	NPV
Voucher Cost	−200	0	0		
Increased Earnings	0	20	0		
Health Benefits	0	5	100		
Net Private Benefit	−200	25	100	13%	£213.53
Voucher Cost	−400	0	0		
Tax Revenue	0	2	0		
Reduced Crime / Health Costs	0	20	20		
Net Social Benefit	−600	47	120	8%	£156.19

As can be seen from the above exercise, changing the initial conditions (Table 6.2) causes a large change in both the NPV and the IRR, whereas changing later conditions (Table 6.3) causes a large change in the NPV only. This is because of the non-linear relationship between both the NPV and IRR and the distribution of the stream of future benefits.

CONCLUSION: THE USES AND ABUSES OF CBA

In this chapter we have shown how the statistical relationships identified through the impact study could be converted into monetary values and worked into a CBA. We have explained how it would be possible to attach values not only to income, employment, taxes and benefit savings but also to the wider benefits of learning such as health improvements and crime reduction. Table 6.4 summarises the private and external benefits and costs which have been referred to in this chapter. This table is not exhaustive, in particular about the external benefits of learning, but provides a guide to what has been enumerated elsewhere.

Table 6.4 **A summary of potential benefits and costs of lifelong learning**

	Private	External
Benefits	Increased earnings Improved employment prospects Improved health	Exchequer savings Reduction in crime Economic growth
Costs	Direct costs of lifelong learning Forgone earnings	Exchequer costs Over-education (Qualification inflation)

The results of CBA could then be expressed either in terms of a percentage rate of return (IRR) or a monetary value (NPV), or both. We conclude by commenting on how these results could be used and with a cautionary note about some of the problems with, and possible abuses of, CBA as an evaluation tool.

By comparing the results of CBA with the returns or present values of alternative expenditures, judgements can be made as to the efficiency with which money is being invested. In theory, investment in the project with the highest social rate of return or present value will be the most efficient from the perspective of society. Usually, though, the government will have to choose between a number of competing lifelong learning projects and use CBA to assess the relative efficiency of each with the minimum criterion for project acceptance being a social rate of return of at least 6 per cent or a positive Net Present Value if the Green Book discount rate of 6 per cent is used.

An assessment of the efficiency of regional or institutional expenditure may also be conducted through the use of CBA. In the example of the voucher scheme, an assessment of the social rate of return to expenditure of each authority could be conducted. Of course, subjects studied and labour market differences will make a large difference to rates of return and this must be taken into account if valid comparisons are to be made.

CBA has obvious appeal to policy makers in terms of accountability and providing a common monetary benchmark for making decisions. However, a number of caveats should be made about the interpretation and use of results. Firstly, there are a number of intangible costs and benefits which would be extremely difficult to express as monetary values. From the individual perspective, it is uncommon to include the *consumption benefits* of education in CBA. One of the major private benefits arising from lifelong learning might be the enjoyment of the course and the future utility arising from leisure in terms of the aesthetic appreciation of cultural activities, or in increased job satisfaction at work. More significantly, it is difficult to place a monetary value on outputs such as social capital, discussed in Chapter 3, although Knack and Keefer (1997) provide tentative evidence about the correlation between measures of trust and economic growth.

In terms of costs, it might be difficult to place a precise economic valuation on time expended in learning. It is common to include only income forgone as a measure of an estimate of the time spent in education but some learning does not require the sacrifice of income. In addition, problems may arise in imputing direct costs into a rate of return analysis. It is frequently assumed that these are additional costs which would not be paid unless the individual were in education. However, these costs are only additional to the costs associated with the forgone activity. For example, the direct costs associated with working may also include travel and expenses that in extreme cases could outweigh the direct costs of education.

Second, there may be data problems. It is assumed that age-earnings profiles are based on longitudinal data. However, in practice, cross-sectional data are often used. These data may be unduly influenced by short-run cyclical changes in the business cycle and they cannot account for future changes in demand and supply for educated manpower. Additionally, it might be difficult to gain information on the external benefits and costs of education through the life cycle.

Third, even if the above two problems can be overcome, there are difficulties in the interpretation of CBA. CBAs of learning are based on the assumption that it is the investment in learning that is yielding the return. However, the screening hypothesis holds that education does not increase the productive capacity of individuals but rather acts to identify individuals with certain levels of productivity. In other words, there is *self-selection* in education (Chapters 4 and 5). In addition, it is difficult to isolate the benefits attributable to lifelong learning from those of previous education. Although education may have a useful economic function in terms of selection, the existence of screening might mean that the private and social returns to education are overstated. The effects of screening can sometimes be estimated through statistical modelling techniques (see Chapter 5). Screening also has implications in terms of the assessment of the impact of education on economic output. It is frequently assumed in rate of return analysis that earnings are related to productivity. However, if education has a screening function then it may account for only a fraction of the improvement in total output.

Finally, even in the absence of screening, CBA alone is an insufficient criterion for policy judgements. CBA is at best a 'lagged' indicator for the direction of policy, revealing the direction but not the quantity of investment in learning that should occur. Policy makers need to take into account the impact of a further expansion of learning on the existing benefits of education. Returns to education are likely to be depressed following an increase in the supply of trained workers. Policy makers must also be aware that the technique of CBA heavily discounts the value of projects that realise a stream of benefits far in the future, for example, those which yield benefits after retirement or for succeeding generations. Discounting benefit streams is fundamental to CBA. However, for policy purposes, alternative indicators such as those measuring quality of life could be used alongside CBA in evaluating projects with late benefit streams.

Chapter 7

Conclusions and Recommendations

This report sets out different ways to approach the evaluation of lifelong learning interventions. In this final chapter, we draw out the main themes and end with a series of guidelines that potential evaluators, and those assessing evaluation proposals, need to consider. We stress that these are simply guidelines and not prescriptions: there is no uniformly best way of doing an evaluation and approaches are bound to vary according to the nature of the intervention. We do, nevertheless, believe that there are a number of issues that any evaluation design needs to address.

Evaluation is a broad topic, eclectic in the sense that it draws on all the disciplines in social science, with a vast and widely spread literature. This report is not so ambitious as to try to cover all its aspects. Instead, we have restricted ourselves to those aspects of evaluation that are applicable when an intervention, typically but not necessarily emanating from government, is applied in a selective rather than in a universal way. In addition, we have contextualised our ideas within the class of potential interventions that could be directed at increasing lifelong learning and generating wider benefits from it. Furthermore, the focus of the report is essentially technical, although by no means solely quantitative. It is concerned with questions of measurement, sampling, experimental design, understanding processes, estimating and causally attributing impacts, and assessing costs and benefits.

Within this framework we have distinguished evaluation from monitoring and modelling. We have shown that the areas of provision which are most amenable to evaluation are those where comparisons can be made between similar groups with differing levels of exposure to the intervention in question. Where provision is essentially universal (such as the National Curriculum), then monitoring would generally be a more suitable activity. For most of the activities falling under the heading of post-compulsory education, the problems of self-selection mean that modelling is more appropriate. Evaluation is best suited to those activities where exposure to the intervention is restricted or differentiated. For example, interventions taking place in some LEAs, or under the auspices of some LSCs and not others, where demand for courses exceeds supply, or for initiatives introduced in experimental or pilot forms such as Education Maintenance Allowances.

The question of who owns the evaluation is an important one. This is an issue that goes beyond the technical issues that are the primary subject of this report. Nevertheless, an evaluation cannot hope to succeed without the cooperation of all its stakeholders – teachers, learners, administrators and so on. All these groups need to feel included in the processes that lead to an evaluation design, and to feel that they are being consulted as appropriate at all subsequent stages. This is not primarily an issue of method – there are dangers of an evaluation being seen as oppressive whatever approach is being used. A more quantitative approach is, however, a less familiar one to some involved in delivering lifelong learning and might therefore need to be explained especially carefully.

The need for evaluations to cover both implementation and impact has been stressed throughout. Moreover, evaluators need to relate implementation to impact through reference to theories of change. In essence, evaluation as set out here is about finding out whether an intervention leads to changes, how large the changes are, whether they are uniform across groups, and how and why the changes took place, perhaps more markedly in some settings than in others.

Impact evaluations which do not use controls in the design lead to possible biases of self-selection, and there is a strong ethical case to be made in favour of randomisation. Longitudinal data are particularly valuable as some benefits of lifelong learning might not fully emerge until some time after the intervention has ended. Sample size, number and timing of measurement occasions, and attrition are all important issues. Multilevel modelling techniques can be used to show impacts at various levels of a hierarchy over time.

The outcomes of lifelong learning can be portrayed as forms of capital at the individual (human capital), familial (cultural capital) and meso-economic (social and intellectual capital) levels. Identity capital spans human, cultural and social capital. At the macro-economic level, there may be impacts for the exchequer and general economic growth. Not all outcomes can be placed in a capital or economic context and quality of life represents an alternative approach to outcome measurement.

Cost-benefit analysis (CBA) is dependent upon the validity of the impact study. Techniques of CBA have advanced so that we may now place a monetary value on the wider benefits of learning such as tax and welfare benefit savings, health and reductions in crime as well as more traditional benefits such as increases in income. However, there are difficulties in both measuring and interpreting the costs and benefits of lifelong learning. Evaluators should be careful to state both assumptions and methods of calculation. CBA could benefit from collaboration between research centres and government. Issues such as placing a monetary value on wider benefits and estimating the tax, benefit and economic growth implications of lifelong learning are potential areas for collaborative work.

Here we set out a number of key topics that we believe need to be addressed in all evaluation designs. They should inform not only the design and assessment of evaluations, but also the processes that lead to an evaluation being considered in the first place. We refer to the relevant sections where these topics are covered in detail.

1) Evaluation must be seen as a planned activity, built into interventions from the outset, and timed in such a way that appropriate designs can be used, and appropriate data analyses carried out (Chapter 1). Moreover, proper evaluation is not cheap – the level of resources required needs careful consideration.

2) The target population for the evaluation needs to be clearly defined in both space and time (Chapter 4).

3) Evaluations should cover both implementation and impact, and the links between them, using whatever research methods are appropriate (Chapter 2).

4) Heterogeneity is a fundamental characteristic of interventions. They – and hence their effects – vary in form and intensity according to who is delivering them, where they are being delivered and in what context. Those learners receiving the intervention are also heterogeneous and cannot be expected to respond uniformly to it (Chapters 2, 4 and 5).

5) Impact can only be evaluated by making comparisons with those not receiving the intervention (Chapter 4).

6) Randomisation is a powerful way of eliminating at least some of the profound difficulties posed by self-selection. Those designing evaluations should be expected to make the case against randomisation when submitting proposals (pp. 47–50).

7) Interventions aim to affect a range of outcomes at different levels. Hence, a range of measures will usually be needed. Moreover, these outcomes will often be at different levels – the learner, their family, their community and so on. When this is the case, these levels must be sampled (Chapter 4).

8) The range of outcomes measured, at different levels, will often lead to the need to use advanced statistical methods both to measure impact and to model the processes leading to those impacts. Aggregate data will rarely be useful; individual data are nearly always essential (Chapter 5).

9) Impact evaluations need to be concerned with measuring short, medium and long-term effects (p. 18).

10) Evaluation should be a public activity, and the results should be shared amongst all interested parties, and the wider public. It is a collaborative activity – both between evaluators and stakeholders and also across evaluations of different but related interventions.

11) Evaluations need to address the issue of costs and benefits, but also be aware of the limitations of CBA (Chapter 6).

Bibliography

AECDU (1985) *Educational home visiting in an adult education context: an evaluation*, London: ILEA.

Anderson, S. et al. (1980) *Statistical Methods for Comparative Studies*, New York: Wiley.

Angrist, J. and Lavy, V. (1996) *The effect of teen childbearing and single parenthood on childhood disabilities and progress in school (Working Paper 5807)*, New York: N.B.E.R.

Asplund, R. and Pereira, P.(1999) *Returns to Human Capital in Europe*, Helsinki: T.O.

Arrow, K. (1973) 'Higher education as a filter', *Journal of Public Economics*, 2: 193–216.

Bagnall, R. (1990) 'Lifelong education: the institutionalisation of an illiberal and regressive ideology?', *Educational Philosophy and Theory*, 22: 1–7.

Bennett, R., Glennerster, H. and Nevinson, D. (1995) 'Investing in skill: expected returns to vocational studies', *Education Economics*, 3: 99–117.

Bourdieu, P. and Passeron, J. (1990) *Reproduction in Education, Society and Culture*, London: Sage.

Bynner, J. (1998) 'Education and family components of identity in the transition from school to work', *International Journal of Behavioral Development*, 22: 29–53.

Bynner, J., Mcintosh, S., Vignoles, A., Dearden, L., Reed, H and Van Reenan, J. (2001) *Improving Adult Basic Skills: Benefits to the individual and to society*, DfEE Research Report RR251, London: HMSO.

Caldwell, B. (1997) 'A gestalt for the reengineering of school education for the knowledge society', *School Leadership and Management*, 17: 201–215.

Campbell, D.T. (1988) 'The experimenting society', in Overman, E.S. (ed.), *Methodology and Epistemology for Social Science: Selected Papers*: 290–314, Chicago: University of Chicago Press.

Cloonan, M., Hearinger, A., Matarazzo, B., Murphy, M. and Osborne, M. (1999) 'The use of cost-benefit analysis in funding continuing education: steering the fifth wheel', *International Journal of Lifelong Education*, 18: 492–504.

Cohn, E. and Geske, T. (1990), *The Economics of Education*, Oxford: Pergamon Press.

Connell, J.P. and Kubisch, A.C. (1998) 'Applying a theory of change approach to the evaluation of Comprehensive Community Initiatives: progress, prospects and problems' in Fulbright-Anderson, K., Kubisch, A.C., and Connell, J.P. (eds) *New Approaches to Evaluating Community Initiatives. Theory, Measurement and Analysis*, Vol 2, Washington DC: The Aspen Institute.

Cook, T.D., and Campbell, D.T. (1979) *Quasi-Experimentation*, Chicago: Rand McNally.

Côté, J. (1997) 'An empirical test of the identity capital model', *Journal of Adolescence*, 20: 577–597.

Cronbach, L.J. (1982) *Designing Evaluations of Educational and Social Programs*, San Francisco: Jossey-Bass.

DETR (2000) *Local Quality of Life Counts – A Handbook for a Menu of Local Indicators of Sustainable Development*, London: DETR.

DfEE (1998a) *The Learning Age: A Renaissance for a New Britain*, London: HMSO (Cm3270).

— (1998b) *Practice Progress and Value. Learning Communities: Assessing the Value they Add*, London: DfEE.

— (1998c) *Learning Towns, Learning Cities*, London: DfEE.

DfEE Centre for Research on the Wider Benefits of Learning (2000) *Improving Adult Basic Skills*, London: DfEE Centre for Research on the Wider Benefits of Learning.

DSS (2000a) 'Evaluation of the New Deal for Lone Parents' Research Report no.108, London: DSS.

— (2000b) 'Evaluation of the New Deal for Lone Parents' Research Report no.109, London: DSS.

Easton, P. (1997) *Sharpening Our Tools: Improving Evaluation in Adult and Nonformal Education*, Hamburg: UNESCO.

Edwards, J. (1986) *Working Class Adult Education in Liverpool: A radical approach. An evaluation of Second Chance to Learn*, Manchester: University of Manchester.

Estes, R.J. (1998) 'Social development trends in transition economies 1970–95' in Hope, K.R (ed) *Challenges of Transformation and Transition from Centrally Planned to Market Economies*, Nagoya: United Nations.

FEDA (1997) *GNVQs 1993–1997: a National Survey Report*, London: FEDA.

FEFC (2000) Circular 00/06: 'College Performance Indicators 1998–1999 and 1999–2000'.

Gilbert, J.P., Light, R.J. and Mosteller, F. (1975) 'Assessing social innovations', in Bennett, C.A. and Lumsdaine, A.A. (eds) *Evaluation and Experiment*, New York: Academic Press.

Gillborn, D. and Youdell, D. (2000) *Rationing Education: Policy, Practice, Reform and Equity*, Buckingham: Open University Press.

Goldstein, H. (1995) *Multilevel Statistical Models*, London: Edward Arnold.

Groot, W. and Van Den Brink (1997) 'Allocation and the returns to over-education in the U.K.', *Education Economics*, 5: 169–183.

Grootaert, C. (1990) 'Returns to formal and informal education in Côte d'Ivoire: the role of the structure of the labour market', *Economics of Education Review*, 9: 309–319.

HEFCE (1999a) Circular 99/66: 'Performance Indicators in Higher Education'.

— (1999b) Circular 99/11: 'Performance Indicators in Higher Education: First Report of the Performance Indicators Steering Group'.

Heckman, J.J. and Hotz, V.J. (1989) 'Choosing among alternative non-experimental methods for estimating the impact of social programs', *Journal of the American Statistical Association*, 84: 862–874.

Heckman, J. J. and Singer, B. (eds.) (1985) *Longitudinal Analysis of Labor Market Data*, Cambridge: CUP.

Hillage, J., Uden, T., Aldridge, F. and Eccles, J. (2000) 'Adult learning in England: a review. NIACE and IES' (report 369), Brighton: Institute of Employment Studies.

Hodkinson,P. and Sparkes,A. (1994) 'The myth of the market : the negotiation of training in a Youth Credit Pilot Scheme', *British Journal of Education and Work*, 7 (3): 5–19.

Jarvis, P., Holford, J., Griffin, C. and Dubelaar, J. (1997) *Towards the Learning City: An Evaluation of the Corporation of London's Adult Education Voucher Schemes*, London: Corporation of London.

Joint Centre for Longitudinal Research (2000) *Sure Start Evaluation Development Project Report*, London: Joint Centre for Longitudinal Research.

Kenkel, D.S. (1991) 'Health behaviour, health knowledge and schooling'. *Journal of Political Economy*, 99: 287–305.

Kish, L. (1987) *Statistical Design for Research*, New York: Wiley.

Knack, S. and Keefer, P. (1997) 'Does social capital have an economic payoff? A cross-country investigation', *Quarterly Journal of Economics*, 112(4): 1251–1288.

Leney, T., Lucas, N., and Taubman, D. (1998), *Learning Funding: The impact of FEFC funding, evidence from twelve F.E. colleges*, London: NATFHE.

Lochner, K., Kawachi, I. and Kennedy, B. (1999) 'Social Capital: a guide to its measurement', *Health and Place*, 5: 259–270.

McMahon, W. (1997) 'Conceptual framework for measuring the total social and private benefits of education', *International Journal of Educational Research*, 27: 453–481.

— (1998) 'Conceptual framework for the analysis of the social benefits of lifelong learning', *Education Economics*, 6: 309–346.

Mincer, J. (1974) *Schooling, Experience and Earnings*, New York: Colombia University.

Moreland, R. and Lovett, T. (1997) 'Lifelong learning and community development', *International Journal of Lifelong Learning*, 10: 201–216.

Murray, D.M. (1998) *Design and Analysis of Group-Randomized Trials*, New York: OUP.

NACRO (1998) *Wasted Lives: Counting the costs of juvenile offending*, London: NACRO.

National Advisory Council on Adult Education (1978) *An Assessment of the Federal Adult Education Act Program*, Washington D.C.: NACAE.

OECD (1996) *Lifelong Learning For All*, Paris: OECD.
— (1997) *Education Policy Analysis*, Paris: OECD.
— (1998) *Education at a Glance: OECD Indicators*, Paris: OECD.
Orr, L.L. (1999) *Social Experiments: Evaluating public programs with experimental methods*, London: Sage.
Pawson, R. and Tilley, N. (1997) *Realistic Evaluation*: London, Sage.
Payne, J. (1990) *Adult Off-the-job Skills Training: An evaluation study*, Sheffield: Training Agency.
Plewis, I. (1985) *Analysing Change*, Chichester: Wiley.
— (1997) *Statistics in Education*, London: Edward Arnold.
— (2000a) 'Evaluating educational interventions using multilevel growth curves: the case of Reading Recovery', *Educational Research and Evaluation*, 6: 83–101.
— (2000b) Modelling impact heterogeneity, paper presented to Royal Statistical Society Conference: Evaluating Economic and Social Programmes, July 2000.
Plewis, I., and Hurry, J. (1998) 'A multilevel perspective on the design and analysis of intervention studies', *Educational Research and Evaluation*, 4: 13–26.
Psacharopoulos, G. (1995) *Building Human Capital for Better Lives*, Washington D.C.: World Bank.
Rosenbaum, P.R. and Rubin, D.B. (1983) 'The central role of the propensity score in observational studies for causal effects', *Biometrika*, 70: 41–55.
Rossi, P.H. and Freeman, H.E. (1993) *Evaluation: A systematic approach* (5th Edn), Newbury Park, Ca.: Sage.
Scriven, M. (1973) 'Goal free evaluation' in House, E.R. (ed.) *School Evaluation : The politics and process*, Berkeley, Ca: McCutchan.
Schultz, T., (1961) 'Investment in human capital', *American Economic Review*, 51: 1–17.
Schuller, T., Bynner, J., Green, A., Blackwell, L., Hammond, C., Preston, J. and Gough, M. (2001) *Modelling and Measuring the Wider Benefits of Learning: A synthesis*, London: Institute of Education, University of London.
Siemens, C. (1998) *Community Education and Crime Prevention: Confronting foreground and background causes of criminal behavior*, Westport: Bergin and Garvey.
Stufflebeam, D. (1971) *Educational Evaluation and Decision-Making in Education*, cited in Easton (1997) op.cit., pp. 82.

Sudarsky, J. (1999) *Colombia's Social Capital: The National Measurement with the BARCAS*, Wahington D.C.: World Bank.

Toye, J. and Vigor, P. (1994) *Implementing NVQs. The experience of employers, employees and trainees*, Brighton: Institute of Manpower Studies.

United Nations (1993) *Human Development Report 1993*, New York: Oxford University Press.

Westphalen, S. (1999) 'Reporting on human capital ; objectives and trends', Paper presented at an International Symposium on *Measuring and Reporting Intellectual Capital: Experience, Issues and Prospects*, Amsterdam 1999.

Wolfe, B. and Zuvekas, S. (1997) 'Nonmarket outcomes of schooling', *International Journal of Educational Research*, 27: 447–532.

Word, E.R., Johnston, J., Bain, H.P., Fulton, B.D. et al. (1990) *The State of Tennessee's Student/Teacher Achievement Ratio (STAR) Project: Technical Report 1985–1990*, Nashville: Tennessee State University.

APPENDIX 1.1

Data Sources for Monitoring Lifelong Learning

There are two groups of statistics that could be used to monitor lifelong learning:

- education statistics produced by the DfEE and other statutory bodies;
- continuing cross-sectional and longitudinal surveys on education and training. These surveys also cover areas such as health, families and attitudes to civic participation that may be helpful in identifying the wider benefits of learning. Although these surveys can be used for monitoring, their primary use is for modelling.

The Further Education Funding Council (FEFC), Higher Education Statistics Agency (HESA) and the Basic Skills Agency compile statistics on Further Education, Higher Education and basic Adult Education respectively. The Learning and Skills Council (LSC) will be shortly taking over responsibility for provision from the FEFC and the Training and Enterprise Councils (TECs). One of the LSC functions will be to set up a database to track learners, but the details of this database have yet to be agreed.

EDUCATION STATISTICS

Targets for lifelong learning

http://www.dfee.gov.uk/nlt/targets.htm

There are National Learning Targets for individuals and organisations. By 2002 the achievement targets for England are:

- 85 per cent of 19 year olds with a level 2 qualification (5 GCSEs, GNVQ Intermediate or NVQ level 2);
- 60 per cent of 21 year olds with a level 3 qualification (2 A-Levels, GNVQ Advanced or NVQ level 3);
- 50 per cent of adults with a level 3 qualification (as above);
- 28 per cent of adults with a level 4 qualification (degree or higher level vocational qualification);
- 7 per cent reduction in non-learners (the learning participation target);
- 45 per cent of medium sized or larger organizations (those with 50 or more employees) to be recognized as an 'Investor in People';
- 10,000 small organizations (those with 10 to 49 employees) to be recognized as an 'Investor in People'.

Scotland, Wales and Northern Ireland are making their own separate arrangements.

At the national level, the Labour Force Survey (LFS) is used to monitor the levels 2–4 targets for young people and adults. For the Investors in People targets, information is collected through TECs, government offices and Investors in People (UK). The DfEE has yet to decide on a collection strategy for the new learning participation target and how to measure local and regional progress towards levels 2–4 targets for young people and adults.

Further Education statistics

http://www.fefc.ac.uk/data/index.html

The FEFC produces statistics based upon FE college Individualised Student Returns (ISR) covering:

- Recruitment, retention and achievement of FE students by LEA;
- FE students disaggregated by level of qualification, type of qualification, FEFC region, gender, ethnicity, disability, type of provision, level of additional support, major sources of funding, payment of tuition fees;
- College performance indicators.

Higher Education statistics

http://www.hesa.ac.uk/

The Higher Education Statistics Agency (HESA) produces relevant statistics by course of study on:

- students in Higher Education – composition in terms of age, ethnicity, gender and socio-economic status;
- first destinations of graduates and leavers from Higher Education;
- percentage from schools and colleges in the state sector;
- percentage from social classes 'skilled manual', 'semi-skilled', and 'unskilled';
- percentage from low participation neighbourhoods;
- non-continuation rates after first year at institution;
- projected outcomes and efficiency;
- first degree / undergraduate entrants;
- mature full-time undergraduate entrants;
- part-time undergraduate entrants;
- learning outcomes.

Audit Commission

http://www.local-regions.detr.gov.uk/bestvalue/

The Audit Commission produces local authority performance indicators relating to post-compulsory and adult education including:

- the number of enrollments on all adult education courses provided and secured by the local authority per 1000 adult population;
- expenditure per head on adult education provided and secured by the LEA.

Basic Skills Agency

http://www.basic-skills.co.uk/

The Basic Skills Agency collates adult education statistics on:

- number of learners;
- learners by organisation type;
- regional analysis of learners pursuing courses in basic numeracy / literacy.

LONGITUDINAL AND CROSS-SECTIONAL SURVEYS

Youth Cohort Survey

The Youth Cohort Survey (YCS) is a series of longitudinal studies of cohorts of young people reaching the end of compulsory full-time education in England and Wales. Each survey is based on a probability sample of young people, clustered by school. YCS collects information on:
- qualifications gained at the end of year 11 and after;
- economic and training activity;
- labour market activity and earnings;
- reasons for non-participation in education and work;
- careers education and guidance;
- attitudes to education and training;
- time diaries;
- background information, including parental employment and qualifications, housing tenure, household composition and ethnicity.

Labour Force Survey (LFS)

The Labour Force Survey is a repeated cross-sectional survey with a panel element and covers:
- education and training data;
- employment, unemployment and job-search activities;
- labour mobility and travel to work;
- hours of work and health (health problems / disabilities, sickness and accidents).

General Household Survey (GHS)

Another repeated cross-sectional survey including:
- age on leaving school / last place of full-time education;
- distance learning (correspondence / Open University);
- qualifications obtained;
- training courses;
- Further / Higher Education;
- professional qualifications.

In addition, there are many health and disability related questions with respect to general health, infirmity, injury, illness, limit to activities, number of days ill and medical consultations. The GHS does not directly concern itself with attitudes, values or civic participation, being more concerned with behavioural questions which are indirectly related to these topics such as use of contraception, cigarette smoking, cohabitation, marriage and divorce, living arrangements, private health care, and consumption of alcohol.

British Household Panel Study (BHPS)

This is a longitudinal study and therefore probably more useful for modelling rather than monitoring. It covers:
* training / purposes of training;
* Further / Higher education;
* qualification level and type.

It also produces data on health, use of health provision and accidents. In addition, there are forty questions in the survey, related to values, attitudes and civic participation.

British Social Attitudes Survey (BSA)

A repeated cross-sectional survey that identifies attitudes to:
* civil liberties;
* crime;
* education;
* employment;
* health;
* local government;
* moral values;
* social security;
* taxation.

National Child Development Study (NCDS)

The National Child Development Study is a continuing longitudinal study which aims to follow the lives of all those living in Great Britain who were born in one week in 1958. There have been six sweeps of this study to date, and the sixth gathered information on those aged 41/42. The study has gathered a wide range of information on educational qualifications, and on individuals' social, physical and economic development.

British Cohort Study (BCS70)

The British Cohort Study began in 1970 and there have been five sweeps of this longitudinal study. Like the NCDS, this study also gathers information on education, social and physical development and economic status.

National Adult Learning Survey (NALS)

The 1997 NALS aimed to identify the extent to which people were taking part in different types of learning, reasons for taking part in learning and the costs and perceived benefits of participation. Follow-up surveys are to have a panel element.

Appendix 2.1 **Systems representation of a lifelong learning programme**

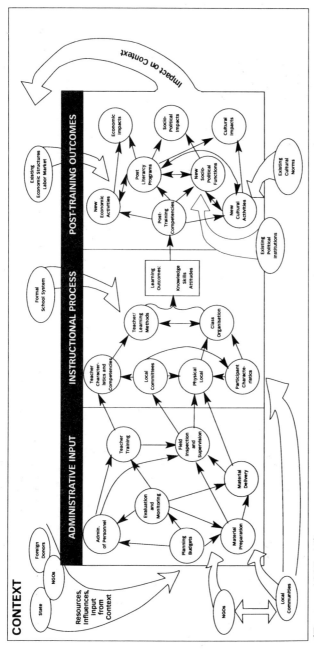

(Easton, 1997: 65)

The diagram shows the relationship between various inputs, processes and outcomes of a lifelong learning programme. As well as displaying the links between programme elements, the diagram also illustrates the interaction between the intervention and the wider context.

Appendix 2.2 Stufflebeam scheme of evaluation comparisons

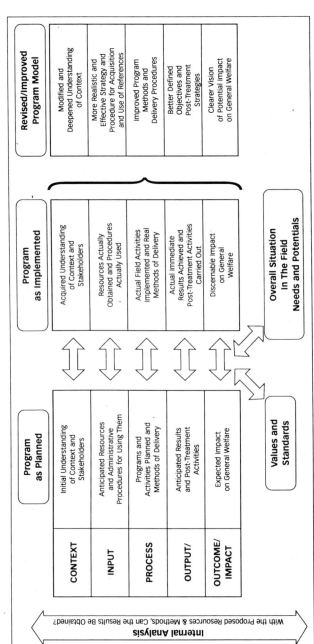

	Program as Planned	Program as Implemented	Revised/Improved Program Model
CONTEXT	Initial Understanding of Context and Stakeholders	Acquired Understanding of Context and Stakeholders	Modified and Deepened Understanding of Context
INPUT	Anticipated Resources and Administrative Procedures for Using Them	Resources Actually Obtained and Procedures Actually Used	More Realistic and Effective Strategy and Procedure for Acquisition and Use of References
PROCESS	Programs and Activities Planned and Methods of Delivery	Actual Field Activities Implemented and Real Methods of Delivery	Improved Program Methods and Delivery Procedures
OUTPUT/	Anticipated Results and Post-Treatment Activities	Actual Immediate Results Achieved and Post-Treatment Activities Carried Out	Better Defined Objectives and Post-Treatment Strategies
OUTCOME/ IMPACT	Expected Impact on General Welfare	Discernable Impact on General Welfare	Clearer Vision of Potential Impact on General Welfare

Values and Standards

Overall Situation In The Field Needs and Potentials

Internal Analysis
With the Proposed Resources & Methods, Can the Results Be Obtained?

(Easton, 1997: 79)

The diagram shows how comparing the planned and the implemented programme may lead to modification. Comparisons are undertaken for each element of the system (context, input, process, output, and outcome). The process of evaluation is therefore seen as continuous and formative, with evaluation results feeding back into the programme structure.